AF470672

FIENNES ON RAILS

Have you heard the story about the General Manager and the Bishop? The General Manager was Gerry Fiennes and the Bishop Eric Treacy, between them driving *Matthew Murray* on the Middleton Railway, Leeds. What happened is described on page 189.

FIENNES
ON RAILS

Fifty years of railways
as seen by

GERARD FIENNES

Former General Manager BR Western Region;
BR Eastern Region; Chief Operating Officer BRB

DAVID & CHARLES
Newton Abbot   London   North Pomfret (Vt)

British Library Cataloguing in Publication Data

Fiennes, Gerard
    Fiennes on rails: fifity years of railways.
    1. Railways – Great Britain – History
    – 20th century
    I. Title
    385'.092'4   HE5018

    ISBN 0–7153–8926–2

Photoset in Linotron Trump Mediaeval by
Northern Phototypesetting Co, Bolton
and printed in Great Britain
by Butler & Tanner Limited, Frome and London
for David & Charles Publishers plc
Brunel House Newton Abbot Devon

Published in the United States of America
by David & Charles Inc
North Pomfret Vermont 05053 USA

Contents

Introduction

'Gerry Fiennes came with a reputation for making friends, dropping the occasional brick, and getting things done.' That was my Press comment when he was sacked as general manager of the Eastern Region for being too outspoken in his *I Tried To Run A Railway*. The man who sacked him, successor to the infamous Dr Beeching, was Stanley Raymond, who had been Gerry's unpopular predecessor at the Western Region at Paddington. And it was during his Western incumbency that I was privileged to know Gerry, whose departure for the Eastern indeed caused us much disappointment in the Westcountry. For the record, a month after dismissing Gerry, Raymond was dismissed by Barbara Castle, the Minister of Transport, who was then shortly dismissed by Harold Wilson. And when Fiennes and Raymond found themselves aboard the Australian-bound *Canberra* for six weeks, it was perhaps inevitable that the former's overtures were not welcome.

Gerry's cutting through the cackle, quickly getting to the vital point – which he tackled with enthusiasm – and his quick-witted balance of humour and sarcasm, were bound to make him occasional enemies as well as many friends. Nobody doubted that he was a true railwayman. He had a deep respect for most working railwaymen doing their tasks faithfully in a long and honourable tradition, and knew how to do most of them from personal experience, for he had fought his way up the ranks. In turn, thousands of railwaymen, and many of us in the greater railway world, adored him, though in truth were not surprised when he put his foot in it because we had seen him do that before. It was all part of his impatient desire to get things done.

He was always looking for new ideas to keep the wheels moving more smoothly, to get trains loaded more quickly (and fully), and to enhance the railway environment. So he listened to all of us . . . including the signalman who denied that he could be the general manager because Gerry had walked to the box and general managers 'don't walk'. He would telephone journalists without telling his public relations people and invite their comment and enthusiasm. He rattled off cheerie, penetrating memos from Brunel's old office at Paddington, keeping everyone on his toes, making everyone feel that extra effort was worthwhile and that everyone was special.

They were, of course, difficult days for the railways, and Gerry had grave misgivings about the policy laid down by Beeching of losing not merely much feeder traffic from the withering branch lines and rural systems, but much wagon-load freight on main lines, since all was now supposed to be concentrated on the new Liner Trains. As the pages that follow tell us, Gerry had a great desire to see longer trains with less marshalling and more mechanisation (and was certainly no friend of traditional steam power for the practical modern railway, though he *did* have room for enthusiasts), but agonised about how any business could thrive while losing so much of its turnover.

But all his railway days had been difficult ones. Traffic was none too abundant on the London & North Eastern when he learnt his trade (assiduously committing his learning to paper) in the Depression; he started in 1929 itself. Then came the war with too much traffic as well as disruptions, and crisis periods such as the fuel shortage of 1947 continuing well afterwards. Always special exertions, breaking through the red tape to get things moving.

In the wilderness after early retirement, Gerry wrote occasional articles, gave a series of Radio Three talks on railway work (a few, adapted, are included in these pages), and enjoyed life and hobbies (especially sailing) at Aldburgh. He once came from there to Newton Abbot just for a David & Charles lunch, but later visits both ways were more leisurely family affairs, not specially about railways, though the very special conversations usually were . . . of the days when everyone and everything depended on getting the trains through, of the great characters railway working threw up, and alas also of the opportunities British Rail lost and deteriorating *esprit de corps*. Gerry was a man of his age, the age in which railways were in the centre of things and he in the centre of them. A household name in the lives of railwaymen of all ranks, he enjoyed his social contacts as much as the challenge of railway work. We often talked about another book capturing the spirit of that work, and happily he completed it – much helped by wise wife Jean – before his death last year.

To read these pages is to get to know an outstanding railwayman and realise (often through the incidentals) something of what our railways were and what was needed to keep them running against climatic, mechanical, human and other odds. The book was written with great enjoyment, though the last part from bed within days of his death, and is a pleasure to publish in the memory of a great friend and railwayman.

David St John Thomas
April 1986

1

An Introduction to Railways

TRAVEL WITH FATHER

At the time of this journey, 1915, Father was fifty-two. He had married late in life so that I, the eldest, was nine. After me there was a gap owing to mother dropping the ball when running for the line; so the rest were five, two and a baby. We always had two holidays a year; in the spring at Bognor in a boarding house; in August in a villa at Dymchurch. Yes, we were privileged. Father was a journalist in the top fifty anyway, as editor of a London Evening and naval correspondent of *The Observer* at the time when we were building sixteen battleships to Germany's ten and an enormous fleet of cruisers and destroyers besides. I don't object to a lot of privilege myself. ASLEF for instance is an élite and should be kept as such because the only railwayman who positively gets us from start to journey's end is the driver. Jean takes issue with me about this but when it comes down to it, what she really objects to is that I had my baths in front of my bedroom fire in a copper tub, warmed and scrubbed by domestics (house guests used to have to be shewn Master Gerard in his bath) while she, the Headmaster's daughter, was bathed in the copper after the washing. Anyway we concede that in holidays we were privileged.

The second fact to be remembered throughout is that Father, normally a large, comfortable, benign *pater familias* had a profound and continued distrust of railways. When, five years after he died, I went during my training to Marylebone he was still remembered as the most persistent and vitriolic hammer of management among the many critics which they had. The first defence against this untrustworthiness was the Count. In those days when you took a house at the seaside

11

you took with you sheets and pillowcases, towels and silver and glass, not to mention a mass of clothing. These were packed in enormous round-topped trunks, hold-alls, cricket bag, hat boxes. One of mother's hatboxes stands at the top of our cellar steps. It is a leather cube about two feet each way. The only handle is in the middle of the lid, which ensures that when you lug it along the sharp edge at the bottom agonisingly bangs against your ankle at every other step. We have not moved it for fifteen years. However, the Count started with the personnel. So Mother and Father, four children, Nurse Gladys Metzgor, Annie the cook and a do-it-yourself girl whose name I have forgotten and twenty-six pieces of luggage – thirty-five in all.

All were assembled on the front of the Rectory at Silchester, West of Reading, where Grandfather was the Rector. The two station flys crunched up followed by a farm wagon. We loaded and crunched and rattled our way to Mortimer station. The stationmaster had recruited an extra porter for the occasion, made the mistake of unloading on to two four-wheeled barrows and sending one toward where the front van would be. This would have frustrated the Count so Father, two shades darker in colour, made his wishes clear. Thirty-five was still the number. The train ran in. Our reserved compartment was full of laughing, bouncing plebs. The stationmaster invited father to an empty compartment further up the train. But there was a compartment with our name on it. It took about fifteen minutes to evict the happy throng. I do not suppose the stationmaster ever gave right-away with greater relief.

The next transfer was at Paddington. In the 1892 Great Northern Railway Rule Book – and I expect those of the other railways were similar – it was provided in Rules 10 and 23 that no servant of the Company must solicit or accept a gratuity, that porters must before the arrival of a train space themselves evenly along the platform, that they must not move until the train came to rest and on no account must they ride on the footboards. Father had a short way with this. As the train ran in he lowered the window, protruded like a snail, looked commanding and opulent, and shouted 'Porter!'. Invariably this produced several riding on footboards and a rolling wave of running, jostling humanity on the platform outside. When the train stopped we assembled by the van. The porters, selected for strength, unloaded. And Father proceeded to the Count.

Then came the crowning glory. On a corner of the Paddington Lawn stood our Horse Bus. Resplendent in scrolls of scarlet and gold, the coachman in a tall hat with a cockade, a patient horse nozzling its nosebag.

I went to the horse's head and made much of him, and – oh glory – was rewarded by an invitation to ride with the coachman on his box and to hold but not to use the whip. We set off through the opulent streets between Paddington and Hyde Park. Often we trundled over stretches of straw or tan bark. It was in those days medical opinion that if someone was seriously ill he or she was to be protected from noise by shutting all the windows and laying down sound-deadening material in the street. Probably some of them were none the worse. On through the Park, Constitution Hill, Buckingham Palace, The Mall, Northumberland Avenue, the Embankment, London Bridge and turn left into the station. Here Father ran into his second difficulty. The porters on the front were weedy little men. Father refused to employ them. But they were wearing red ties and NUR badges and were not going to be done out of their rights. Surprisingly instead of turning puce and shouting Father smiled on them, said we would need three four-wheeled barrows and led them to the trunks. They vanished like a puff of smoke. Others came running. And in due course we proceeded to the Count.

You must remember that this was a Saturday in August. At London Bridge the South Eastern & Chatham Railway was running about forty minutes late. Therefore each platform had three train loads of passengers on hand. Here we came to another foible of Father's, born of his distrust. He would not embark on a train unless there was a general consensus of railwaymen that it was going where he wanted to go. Our porters were broken reeds; the stationmaster towering above the throng in his top hat was surrounded by a dense mob all shouting questions. Eventually the third or fourth ticket collector on a barrier said 'Yes. The Dover train would be the third one on this platform.' So we pushed our way through.

Nevertheless there was not yet a consensus. So Father, maybe bemused by the events so far, said to the guard of the train in the platform: 'Does this train go to Dover?' and, naturally, received the classic answer: 'If I wanted to go there I would not start from here.' However the Foreman on the platform and the Driver also did not think that the train was going to Dover. We – I always tagged along with Father – received similar answers about the second train. Then – oh joy, oh rapture unconfined – the third train drew in and on it was our reserved compartment. Nevertheless Father went around in order to achieve his consensus. Only when the Driver said 'Yes, he was going to Dover and would stop at Sandling Junction for Hythe for us', Father took his Count and we embarked.

We expected that we were now beyond catastrophe. But soon after we started Mother felt faint. There was no corridor, no lavatory. Father fanned her vigorously but ineffectively with his straw hat. Then Nurse Gladys Metzgor spoke for the first and last time – on the principle I suppose that servants should be seen and not heard: 'Burn feathers under her nose' she said and then shut her rat-trap mouth. This sounds crazy. Where today on a train, other than a sleeper, would one find a feather. Then, nothing easier. Mother's hat, Nurse Gladys's, Annie's, were bobbing with fruit and waving with feathers. In a couple of seconds there were feathers. Father, pipe-smoker, had lucifer matches. And mother was restored to health.

We alighted in due form at Sandling Junction. The main line train departed. The branch train to Hythe for Dymchurch drew in. The Count was still correct. Then Father cried: 'My hat'. He had put it on the rack after fanning Mother. But in these matters railways were to be trusted. They had one and all a nationwide network of telegraph. Even when I came on the railway at just before ten o'clock all the circuits fell silent and at ten precisely Railway Time was flashed the length and breadth of the land and made us the punctual nation which we are. In this case the stationmaster set off at a fast waddle to the signalbox. The hat was on the next train up.

The other principal event which I remember about our August holiday that year was that Father rescued Annie from drowning and received an official visit from the Mayor in robes and the Town Clerk in wig to thank him. Nevertheless he was in principle accident prone on a railway. He attracted Events. I remember once he went to Ireland. Thick fog from Holyhead. The Captain's navigation was inch perfect. He hit the Kish lightship at the entrance to Dublin Bay exactly amidships. After they had got the lot sorted out the crew of the waiting train had an unusually long turn-round. In Father's compartment was a little old lady sobbing bitterly. Father attempted to comfort her. 'Its me son' she sobbed. 'He's the dhriver and he's dhrunk and I heard him say:"Begor – I'll make her *shpin* round Bray Head."

2

Great Eastern in the Thirties

CHAOS AT LIVERPOOL STREET

Yes, chaos at Liverpool Street. My own, individual, particular, self-inflicted chaos. 'There are' said my boss, 'no alibis.' And given the then data in 1930 he was right. Mind you, if the Great Eastern had never built No 20 and had instead electrified to Southend before the Kaiser's war, I could never have caused it. But the Great Eastern *did* build the Decapod, able to accelerate from a standing start to 30 miles an hour in 30 seconds. And just as Sir Nigel Gresley with the A4s put back diesel traction on the main lines for thirty years, so did the Great Eastern put back suburban electrification with the Decapod. Not that they ever used her in regular suburban service. Not that they ever built No 21 and her sisters. They used her to win a political battle and then converted her from a ten-coupled suburban tank engine to an eight coupled freight tender engine, at which she was very little use either. But that is not the point.

The point is that in the 1930s the LNER still used steam for traction everywhere. Logically, if as in my case imprudently, they trained their future managers in the practice of steam traction: 'Traffic Apprentice G. F. Fiennes; Southend Loco, July – September 1931; Stratford Loco, October – December 1931.' Six whole months; cleaning, fitting, boiler-making, boiler-washing, fire-dropping, coaling, firing, Running Foreman's office. Not that I did the six whole months. In October I was suddenly out on the line as a Headquarters' Wagon Inspector. It had only just occurred to me that this act of chaos at Liverpool Street had anything to do with it.

Be that as it may, I spent the July and August of a roasting summer at Southend, largely with a four-pound sledge and a

16

chisel or a tube-expander or a cricket bat in my hand. Cleaning and firedropping and coaling were also muscular pursuits, so that when it came to my fortnight on the footplate I was fighting fit and full of enthusiasm to take engines from Southend to Liverpool Street and back single handed.

In general Southend worked its London services with rebuilt Clauds. Lovely engines they were to look at. A high parallel boiler; great striding four-coupled driving wheels; chimney, steam dome, firebox, cab and tender all in proportions which spelled speed and honesty. And if their hired servants did well the dirty, bonecracking, menial tasks like cleaning, firedropping, boiler-washing and making tubes steamtight, they responded by doing an honest job of work.

Well, on my first Monday out on the road, early turn, I stood and watched and listened. On the Tuesday, likewise. But by the second week when we were on the back shift I had run over a thousand miles on the footplate and considered I was ready for work. I began at the beginning. 8821 had come off repairs, so she was cold. I got there real early, begged the 'shed turning' gang to leave me to it and said to myself: 'What would George Stephenson have done?' Answer, just like Mum. A sheet or two of yesterday's paper, some sticks, a few knobs of coal, a match . . . 'raising steam', it's called. It takes a hell of a long time. I built that fire tenderly, piece by piece, front back and sides; then on top. It was nearly an hour before the gauges were flickering. Then I could use the blower, and the shovel became worthwhile.

When the driver and fireman came on duty an hour before departure I had nearly a hundred pounds of steam in the boiler. 'Done it all yourself?' said Bert. I nodded. They must have thought they had done a complete job on me last week because they took their oilcans and waste and flares and began the mumbo-jumbo of preparing the engine. Soon I was using the injectors. In a little Bert and Harry swung themselves on to the footplate. We trundled slowly to the water tank, got down and turned on. A couple of minutes was enough. A quarter of an hour before we were due away we were whistling for the outlet signal from the loco. Bert backed us smoothly on to our train. I got down on the off side; coupling – screw up tight, vacuum pipe – make sure no twisted washers, no steam heater pipes, duck out into the six foot, clamber back on to the footplate, Bert creating the brake, Harry looking at the steam gauge. She is on the point of blowing off, and suddenly with a roar does so. Injectors, quick. Quietens her in a minute. Almost at once, a whistle, a green flag from the guard, an arm outstretched from the station foreman. Bert looks at the signal – off. He jerks firmly at the regulator. No 8821 coughs sharply into her snifting valve. She moves smoothly forward. Almost at once Bert has to shut off for Prittlewell. Half way down the platform he brakes from maybe 15 miles an hour. Away again, smartly this time and soon because we have only eight on and we are on the coastal plain, we are flying. Bert is using a lot of steam. I am busy with injector and shovel, feeding water into the boiler and boiling it. Hockley, Rochford, Rayleigh, Wickford and then the four miles at 1 in 100 of Billericay Bank.

Harry is watching anxiously now. We have 175 pounds of steam on the gauge. The water in the glass is well up. But this is where skill tells. And all I have is brawn and enthusiasm. The shovel goes unrelentingly right, left, centre, forward right, forward left, right, left. . . . The blinding sweat rolls; the muscles crack. After an age Harry says: 'You can ease up now' and in a few moments Bert shuts off for Billericay. So far so good.

In fact easy now. On to Shenfield, over the short rise to Ingrave. Stop at Brentwood. And no more than a breath of steam all the way down the hill to Liverpool Street. Running the fire down too, till as we ease smoothly into No 13 platform, we have no more than 100 pounds on the gauge.

I take my can of tea off the shelf and drink the lot almost non-stop. Our train slides away from us back to Southend. We amble after it and are turned into the engine dock bitten out of the end of the platform. Bert says: 'We're going to the mess rooms. Look after the engine will you?' which I do. I look professional, so I allow, in jeans, denim jacket, engineman's

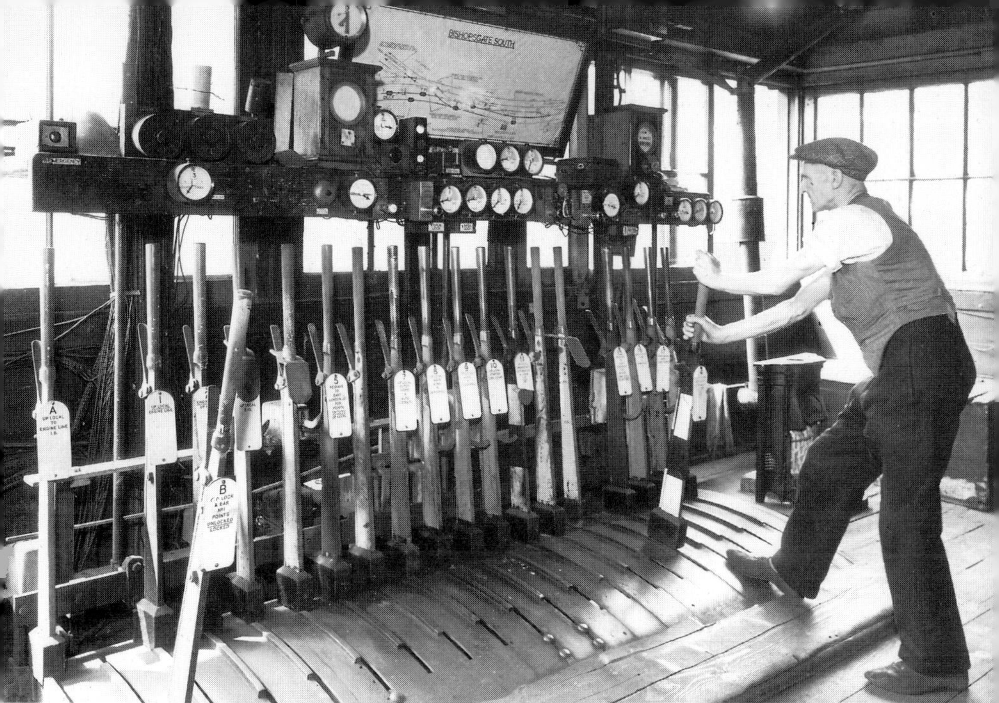

(*above*) Great Eastern signalling – 1 Bishopsgate South controlling the local lines in and out of Liverpool Street carrying the world's most intensive steam suburban service. (*British Railways*) (*overleaf*) Great Eastern signalling – 2 Liverpool Street West, controlling part of one of the busiest stations in the world. Block working was through Sykes lock & block instruments. It lasted until resignalling and electrification of Shenfield services in 1949. (*British Railways*)

cap and sweat rag round my throat. I keep it all on even though the temperature on the footplate must be over 100. On the end of the platform over the rail from my cab are several lads of ages between 10 and 70. I reply to their questions and lecture them a bit on the art of enginemanship. No one asks how long I have been out on the road, so I get by. In the intervals I am, so I think, building a nice bright fire and the gauge up from 100 lbs to 180 or so. Blower on, plenty of shovel, all round, nice and easy on a footplate that is no longer leaping to port and starboard and high in the air, and, of course, showing off to the lads.

I was contentedly sweeping the footplate ready to present Bert and Harry with a prize example of good housekeeping when Bert's voice sounded behind me. 'Cor, blast, lad, what 'ave you *done*?!'

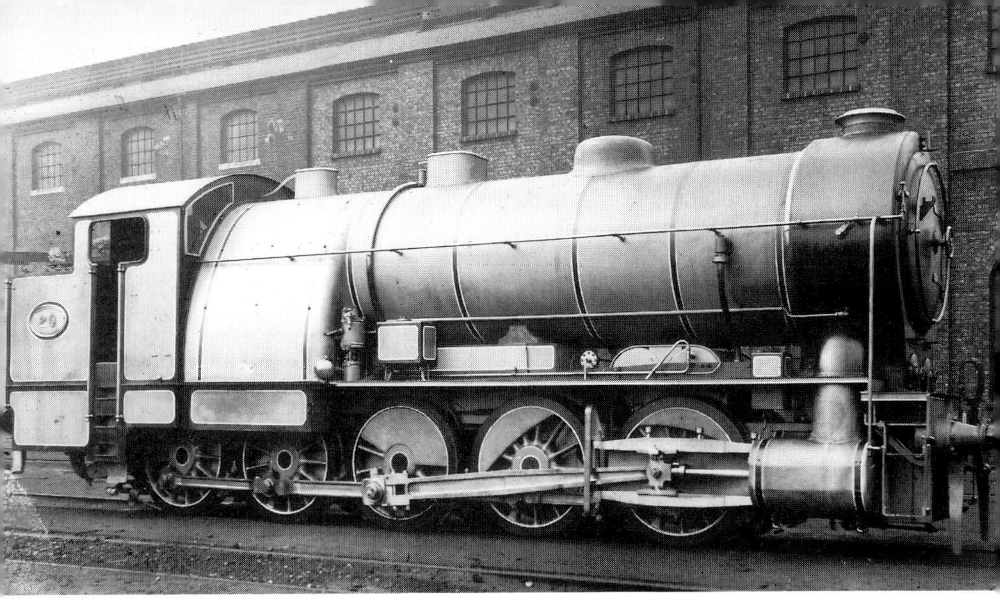

The reason why electrification on the Great Eastern suburban lines was delayed until 1949 – the unique 0–10–0 'Decapod' built in 1920 which proved that steam, in the form of this particular locomotive, could outperform electric trains of the time. (*LNER*)

I turned. From the chimney wreathed slowly, lazily, dark brown coils of smoke drifting all over Liverpool Street. In the firebox no sign of flame; just dead black, over which the smoke whirled toward the tubes. The steam gauge shewed still no more than 100 lb of steam. I retired to a corner and stood in an attitude of utter shame.

Harry took the dart and poked morosely at the ruins. We had eleven minutes before we were due away. In those eleven minutes he had made hardly any impression. We backed on to the train. I summoned enough face to get down and couple up. The starting signal came off with a clang. Bert said: 'Well, let's try' and opened the regulator. We began to drag our weary way out of platform 13 past Liverpool Street East Box and across to the Down Through.

Now the signalmen at Liverpool Street understood these things pretty well in those days. They would ring Bethnal Green West:

'Norwich, or Clacton, or Southend doing bad' and Bethnal Green rings the shunter in Spitalfields yard:

'There'll be one on the Bank any minute.'

The shunter and his Pilot scuttle up to the outlet signal and await the call.

The Southend lumbers round the curve at the foot of the Bank. The beats of his oily exhaust come slowly and more slowly. He grinds to a halt. The fireman gets down and walks towards the Box. The Pilot nips out of the yard and sets back facing road. The fireman gets onto the footplate and conducts it back on to the train. The very junior fireman on the Pilot is making the face of the very senior fireman from Southend as red as he can in the time about 'what a way to run a railway'.

They couple on. The pilot drags the whole enterprise up the Bank, detaches and nips back into Spitalfields Yard. Standard elapsed time for the job — seventeen minutes. Pretty smart. In that seventeen minutes six trains could not get out of Liverpool Street on the Down Through; therefore six up trains were waiting platforms. Something over ten thousand people gnawing the knobs of their umbrellas.

We lumbered dismally away from Bethnal Green. On the way home, Harry firing, Bert said:

'Take the hammer, lad; crack as much coal as you can into dust.'

And so, not knowing what I was about, I did. We were met on arrival by the Shed Master.

'Bert, what the hell have you been up to? Liverpool Street's been a shambles.'

'Bad coal' said Bert, laconically, 'Look at it.' And indeed I had made a creditable heap of dust toward the front of the tender. It was a pity that the handle of the hammer was sticking so obviously out of my pocket.

The headline 'Chaos at Liverpool Street' is one which the London evening papers keep as a standard print. I have always thought that they might, even with their limited vocabulary, vary the words now and again. I have also always thought that the faults for this particular small irregularity in the service were firstly the one of James Holden for designing the Decapod; and secondly, let's face it, mine.

MASHER

I rose from the Chief Controller's seat and drifted negligently toward No 1 Section where Fred West had removed his earphones. Unlike poor Harry Clarke who sat on the next section to him and spent a great deal of his time with his head in his hands hoping *not* to have to control, Fred West's normal attitude was sitting back in his chair, relaxed, master of all he surveyed. And he did survey it. He had a picture in his mind not only where every train or engine on his section was at the moment but where it would be ten . . . twenty . . . thirty minutes hence – by kind permission of the Locomotive Department of course. He was the best controller I have had the luck to meet. When Fred needed to think he removed his headphones and cocked his windcutter face and hooked nose in the air. In half a minute on went the phones, out went his right hand to his selector board, a ring to a signalbox or two: 'do this . . . do that . . . do the other' and Fred would resume his normal posture.

On this occasion as I drifted behind him he rang Whittlesford and said: 'Pull off Main Line for the truck train. The express is at Audley End but he'll never see him.' Then he turned to me and said the one word: 'Masher'. And all was made clear. Masher was – we are in the 1930s now – a driver at March, which was the depot for Whitemoor marshalling yard. The Depot worked trains all over East Anglia, to London, Chelmsford, Colchester, Ipswich, Norwich and Lynn and westward to Doncaster, York, Sheffield, Nottingham, Peterborough. The Drivers had an enormous knowledge of 'roads' and although they had no regular turns to the seaside, Cromer, Yarmouth, Clacton, they signed the book cheerfully enough. Well, if you were offered a day at the seaside with your family and pay for driving the train there and back, wouldn't you chance your arm? As far as I remember, nothing untoward ever happened. And, so far as I was concerned, there was a train, an engine, a driver and a fireman. The Driver had not asked for a Pilotman from Colchester to Clacton. So. . . . Masher was well versed in this art and many others including having a way with the Gresley O2s; well, several ways because the shifts and devices to which he went to fail the engine if it was an O2 allocated to him were legion; and he was not beyond missing a distant or two so that he could be behind an up express instead of in front at Chesterton Junction and so by the time he reached Temple Mills have a couple of comfortable hours overtime under his belt. This let me tell our honest, gentle and unsophisticated readers, was not an uncommon practice on railways. I used to grind my teeth at it but rarely succeeded in doing anything useful about it.

Nevertheless, about Masher May you could be absolutely and beyond peradventure sure of one thing. If he was on the front end of a truck train (empty coal wagons to you non-swedies) on a Saturday and March Town was playing at home you shunted him at your peril.

Now when Fred West told the signalman at Whittlesford to pull off Main Line he was taking two risks. The first one was that Masher would delay the express behind him. This was a calculable risk. The express was two block sections behind and not gaining. If Fred saw to it that Masher had all signals off, not through the goods lines at Cambridge but through the platform, the risk was one of hats blown off, umbrellas turned inside out.

The other risk was that in those far-off days we were supposed to stop goods trains for examination every forty miles or so. And Whittlesford was equipped with four Goods Loops, two up and two down, examiners and lads with buckets full of grease for that purpose. In those days more than half of the coal wagons had grease axle-boxes. The lads used to top them up with a sort of spatula, stuffing the grease hard down in the box. All the same, we got a lot of hot-boxes. This never worried me. Detection was so easy and far in advance of any danger. First, when a box got really warm a little dribble of pallid smoke began to drift along the train. This foul aroma could not fail to be smelt by the guard nor seen by a signalman. Secondly if both came to the conclusion that they would let the train run on and not stop it to detach the wagon, the box burst into flames. Still no danger. The flames shewed that there was still grease in the box. Finally the flames guttered out and the dry journal was turning in a dry axle-box. Then the journal burned through; the corner of the wagon dropped on to the permanent way; and all the wagons behind frolicked over the top. I remember this happening once only with a coal train near Bury St Edmunds. Then thirty wagons of coal ended up at the bottom of an embankment. Thanks to the activities of the honest citizens of Bury we had very little coal to salvage nor indeed the floor boards of the wagons.

It looked as if Fred's decisions were going to plan. I said to the Deputy Chief Controller: 'I am going down. This could be good.' So I betook myself across the station yard and to the country end of the platform. Barnwell Junction's outer and inner distants were off. The station announcer was saying with typical LNER understatement: 'The next train is not a passenger train. Please stand back from the edge of the platform.' Then she was on us. A roar, a snorting, pounding, shouldering, rolling-as-in-a-seaway J39. The long line of wagons streaked unsteadily by with at least half of the brake handles out of their sockets, the brake blocks jumping crazily on the tyres. There was a mighty rushing wind which scattered hats and empty refreshment room cartons. I noticed that the guard had used his three-link coupling to attach his brake van to the last wagon. If he had used his screw-coupling he would have had at least one wagon to keep him slightly steadier. No sign of the guard; probably down on his knees holding grimly to the brake wheel, at prayer. As he went by Masher, cap on the back of his head, lifted a hand to me. A mistake. He was promptly bounced off his seat. I replied with a gesture common then among railwaymen and later popularised by Churchill. I had what I imagine was a response two hundred yards later by a puff of smoke from the chimney. Masher must have said something to his fireman about getting stuck in.

I waited for the express to arrive, some seven minutes later and to time, meanwhile picking up debris. After the stop for five minutes away she went. By that time Masher would be out of reach.

I made my way back across the yard and up the two flights of wooden outside stairs which led to the granary converted into a control in 1927. Over our heads were great chamfered beams, keeping walls apart, or together; from them sprang verticals which soared into the darkness to keep the roof intact. There was one window only – where the door came in. The southern wall was lined with the controllers' desks. The western wall held the 'Fonofore'. This was our only direct link with Stratford control. If, as was naturally frequent, you wanted to speak to them, you lifted the receiver, cranked a handle and after loud static cracklings Donald Duck came on at the other end; except that the quackings, though over-poweringly loud, were completely unintelligible. They sounded like a Mallard duck being harassed by a drake with whom she was on unfriendly terms. Then, mission completed, you wrote in the Log: 'Fonofore unintelligible; natural telephone used ' thereby disarming the critics of our admittedly large telephone bill.

Down the centre of control were three desks; Guards Controller; Deputy Chief Controller; Chief Controller. I went back to my seat and noticed that Fred West was leaning back with a contented expression like a cat into the cream. He looked at that moment very like Harold West, his brother, head shunter at Whitemoor, Norwood Yard. Harold was as wayward a shunter as I knew. A supervisor had to walk down every train which he made up to see that Newcastles didn't get to Nottingham nor Wigans to Hull. But this failing brought him luck. That summer the LNER lost a whole wagon of passengers' luggage in advance destined for Scarborough. After some days they offered a reward of £5, no mean sum in those days, when a head shunter's wages were 65s (£3.25) a week. Harold found the wagon standing as an empty in No 5 road in Norwood yard. It transpired that he had shunted it there himself. No, it hadn't any labels. Yes he had as usual thumped the side to see whether it was an empty. Yes, he got the reward.

So Fred was looking cheerful. He said: 'I've told Chesterton Junction to run Masher via Ely.' This was the shorter, more level route. My eyes travelled on to Harry Clarke. He was in a typical attitude, nose twitching right down on the desk, hands clamped desperately over his ears, dialling and dealing with signalmen who didn't see why their own trains from Ipswich and Norwich should be put inside to clear a royal road for Masher. But they did, and peace reigned until Stonea, three miles from Whitemoor said 'There's a hot box, seventh from the engine, on Masher's train.' Harry took off his headphones and looked round. I said: 'Acknowledge; don't interfere. Hot boxes are the signalman's and guard's business.

Control should very rarely, if ever, interfere in a matter of safety. Control is remote. Controllers are not trained that way. I doubt whether ten per cent of them would pass an examination in rules and regulations. What surprised me was that I intervened almost automatically. The traffic apprentices of the LNER by their training at stations, in marshalling yards, signalboxes, loco depots absorbed not only the crafts consciously but the responses unconsciously. Plenty of railwaymen are the same and I would rather be in the hands of an experienced guard, driver, shunter in a fog or snow or any difficulty than anyone (except a District Inspector) from any District or Head Office. We don't know what they save us from. The sagas are unsung.

Back after my reverie to Harry. He was now heavily engaged with Mossy, the signalman at March East. He was asking and then instructing Mossy to pull off his distants. Mossy never pulled off his distants except for the North Continentals. To do so kept his gates shut against the road for four minutes. This enabled a large gathering of citizens, principally on bicycles. They chi-iked Mossy intolerably. He was a sensitive plant. However, Harry unaccountably prevailed. And Masher, hot box and all, wound his way sedately through the tight curves at March station and so on to Whitemoor Down Hump.

I was recalled to Control by an enveloping aroma of stale

beer and a voice six inches from my right ear bawling: 'Nah, Mister'. Bill Sayers was a first class Deputy Chief Controller. A great bull of a man with a white moon of a face, split horizontally by a short wide bristly moustache, under which lay a gap-toothed mouth in which the remaining teeth were black. 'Nah, Mister' shouted Bill, 'Ah 'ope tha've learnt tha lesson. Never shoont a trook tra-i-n- for an express – not wiv Masher May on t'fro-o-nt – not on a Saturday morning – not when March Tahn are playing at 'ome.'

And do you know, I don't believe I ever did.

LESSONS OF THE WINTER: I

Arthur said: 'Welcome, stranger.' It was January, 1935. The morning had been still. The clouds were low, thick and woolly, like dirty sheep. The glass and our prospects were down in the cellar. Soon after midday there rose a little wayward wind. It blew the first flakes of snow in little wayward circles, round and up and down. The flakes grew large. It was a heavy, warm wet snow. In a couple of hours it was clinging thickly to sleepers and rails and points. It hung on the sagging telephone and block telegraph wires.

Soon the first reports came in. 'No phone block between Newmarket Yard and Snailwell Junction . . . between Elsenham and Stansted . . . between Heacham and Hunstanton . . . between . . . between . . . between . . . Not long after dark we were back to Daniel Gooch, Denison and Huish. We were working trains all over the Cambridge District on the time interval system. Cambridge Control was deaf, speechless and blind to what was happening except through a few Post Office telephones to the larger stations.

'Yardmaster, Whitemoor here.'

'Stanley, what was the last train on the Down?'

'We had the 12.40 Halifax Junction and the 12.5 Newmarket. Haven't seen the rest.'

'So that leaves the Lynn, the Norwich, the Parkeston, the Cambridge somewhere. No sign of the 10.40 Temple Mills?'

'No.'

'Stationmaster Cambridge here.'
'Has the 10.40 Temple Mills gone down?'
'I'll go and find out.'
Pause for 10 minutes while he trudges to Cambridge South
Box. Then:
'10.40 Temple Mills passed at 4.27.'
Three hours ago.

*   *   *

'Stanley, how long since you had a train on the Down?'
'Two hours now.'
'There's a block then. Where are the ploughs?'
'March No 1 is on the joint line to meet Lincoln. No 2 is on
Ely to meet Norwich. We've two light engines keeping the St
Ives loop open.'
I knew that Cambridge were working Up Road to meet
Stratford and the other between Bury and Ely.
'Better not let anything out of the Up Yard till you get one
down and hear what he has to say. Let me know.'
Same instructions to the other yards. On the 'National' to
Lincoln, Stratford, Norwich, Ipswich and the LMS at
Peterborough 'Gosling all freight' Let us get the passengers
home and dried by their tidy wives. Then let us look again.
Funny place a Control, when there is no communication.
The headphones lie on the tables. The pencils and the cards
lie idle. George Mitchell and Harold West are talking in
cathedral undertones. Suddenly Bill Sayers, the Deputy
Chief, rips the silence. Bill is broad and very loud Yorkshire.
'Nah Mister . . . What? . . . 4.15 Lundon not theer yet? . . .
He left 'eer at . . . 6.37. Ar reet, Bob.'
Bob Aggas, Stationmaster at Ely. Find someone with an
engine and go and find this train . . . District Inspectors? Bill
Lewis will be between March and Lynn; George Docking
around Ely North Junction; George Unwin lost in the
direction of Audley End.
I said: 'The Chief Controller's redundant here. I'll go.'
So I rang my newly-wedded wife, told her we weren't
married for the next maybe twenty-four hours which she took

30

with unnecessary aplomb; pulled on my coat, my gum boots, took up my handlamp and picked my way gingerly down the outside stairway from the old granary which was Control. We had been cosy inside. Here it was black dark, hardly a glimmer from the snow. And now it was blowing half a gale. 'There'll be drifting in this' I said to myself.

The station yard was lit; so I made better time through the station and up to Cambridge South.

'Anything about on the Down?'

'That's the 1.55 Temple Mills on the Down Goods; two more behind him, been standing some time.'

'How many on?'

'About fifty-five?'

'O.K. We'll put the train in the yard and go engine and brake to look for the 4.15 London.'

I trudged over to the Down Goods, face low against the blizzard now, knocking the balled snow off my boots on the rails. I clambered on to the Brake and opened the door.

'Welcome, stranger' said Arthur.

'You won't think so presently, boy. We're putting your train in the yard. Then you and I are going engine and brake to look for the 4.15 London somewhere between here and Ely.'

It took us forty minutes to do the job. Rousing the shunters, cleaning the points of snow, labouring across to the Box to tell them what was the next move. When we were ready I was sweating. We drew up to the signal. It came off and we toddled down the Goods line to Coldham's Lane.

'No block between here and Barnwell Junction' said the signalman. 'Proceed at caution.'

'No block between here and Chesterton Junction' said Barnwell. 'Proceed at caution.'

'No block between here and Waterbeach' said Chesterton Junction . . .

We stopped at Waterbeach. 'When did the 4.15 London go down?'

'Over two hours ago.'

'Anything behind him?'

'No.'

'O.K. We'll go and look.'

'No block between here and Stretham Fen. Proceed at caution.'

We doddled on. I was now on the footplate taking turns with the look out. Driver's and fireman's faces were running with melted snow, becoming raw with the stinging wind; eyes bright slits in their faces.

'Stop' I called. A headlight was coming through the snow on the Up Road. I kneed the red shade to the front of my handlamp and waved it from the fireman's side. The light drew along side, and stopped.

'Have you seen the 4.15 London?'

'Half a mile this side of Stretham Fen.'

'Is he in a drift?'

'Nah' in a voice of dreadful scorn. 'You won't get drifting on an embankment. In a cutting, that's different.'

'What's up with him then?'

'Dunno. We didn't stop.' Oh hell.

By this time Arthur was among those present. I was sorry George Unwin wasn't. I was about to break at least two rules and George's motto was 'Do as I say. Don't do as I do.' Arthur would be watching.

I said to the other driver: 'Go on to Waterbeach. Get Wrong Line Orders for both engines. (Fracture No 1) Come through the crossover and behind us on the Down Line. If we can, we'll push him through to Ely. (Fracture No 2) If not, we'll pull him back to Waterbeach.'

Off he went; and on we went. The snow was driving hard and fast, visibility maybe twenty-five yards. We cracked a detonator and in a moment passed a post; Waterbeach Distant. And the fogman standing by his hut. Sooner him than me. His brazier can't have been much use to him in that weather.

'The guard of the London's been back' he told us. 'There's three fogs (detonators) a hundred yards ahead, then another, then one near the rear of the train. He's gone back to the train. Said his passengers were getting umbrageous.'

We set off again. BANG – BANG – BANG. At slow speeds

fogs really do shoot you. BANG. On we went slow. BANG. Down to a crawl. In time the red tail lamp of the London loomed through the snow. We got down on the lee side. Arthur trudged from his brake.

'Arthur' I said, and pointed astern.

''Who? Me? Look, Guv'nor, have a heart.'

'Yes, you, lad. Protect us. That other engine will be up to us before long. Fogs down and pilot him on to us.'

We parted. Arthur's reluctant back faded into the storm. The fireman and I went forward along the lee side of the London. No heads out of the window, asking questions like: 'I am a friend of the Directors and I shall . .' So we arrived at the front end. There was the engine, the driver, the fireman and a black steaming circle in the snow. They had thrown the fire out.

I hauled myself on to the footplate. It was still pretty warm from the faceplate. No one there was incommoded.

'Both injectors failed' said the Driver.

'Will you have enough steam' said I, 'to manage the brake as far as Ely?'

'Doubt it. We've been using what we have to keep the train warm.'

We-ell, what we should do according to the book was to couple the two engines on the rear, push the lot to Stretham Fen, detach one rear engine, let him go through the crossover on to the Up Line, pull the train back past the crossover with the second engine, go through the crossover with the first engine, attach him to the front and proceed in an orderly and legal manner to Ely, not having forgotten to leave the Wrong Line orders with the signalman at Stretham Fen to return by the first up train to Waterbeach, until which no other down train could leave Waterbeach for fear of a head-on collision with two returning engines.

If that sounds complicated to you, it sounded in my head then ruddy well stupid – just as getting two failed injectors on a blasted heath in a blizzard seemed to me stupid also. I stopped the wheels going round and said:

'We'll couple on behind, create a brake and push you to Ely.'

'Don't push too hard, guv'nor. We don't want to land in the river' was all the Driver said.

'You'll have to control the brake. We'll wait till the second engine gets here to help us start.'

I clambered down, remembered my training about public relations and reluctantly climbed into the train. I went through, looking like a Russian with snow on my boots. Nowadays British Railways do it all much better. They would have a public address system, remotely operated by the guard who would have said smoothly: 'This delay has been caused by delay caused by weather conditions. We apologise for any inconvenience caused.' Wanting to get back to Arthur and get on the move I said something like: 'Sorry about all this. We'll be on the move in five minutes and in Ely in half an hour.' This led to all kinds of correspondence with our commercial department, about a roughly-dressed and abrupt young man who would not wait to answer questions. It would have been more if the dining car conductor had not shewn me a sackful of empties whose contents had induced sleep in some and euphoria in others.

At last I hove myself down from the rear Brake. Arthur was at hand with the second engine.

'Give us a start' I said. 'Then take the two wrong line orders back to Waterbeach and let him get the Down Road going again.'

The Driver of our engine wrote 'cancelled' on his order. The Fireman coupled on to the train. We blew the brakes off, whistled a crow loudly and began to move. Still we could see twenty-five yards only. I began to sweat. To push that lot 250 yards long into a main station was likely to be the end of the career of the Chief Controller, Cambridge. On we went. The signalman at Stretham Fen shouted 'No block between here and Ely Dock Junction. Proceed at caution.' I had heard something like this before when I was a year or two younger.

After an age Ely Dock Distant signal crawled by, marked by the fogman's lamp shewing yellow. We came down in speed even more counting the rail joints, 20 yards to a joint. Presently we stopped. Ely Dock Home Signal, we hoped.

Once more the fireman got down and faded into the snow. A long pause. Then he came back.

'When we hear one crow, answer with one crow, blow our brakes off and go ahead. No more than 5mph. The leading engine will stop us in the platform with his brake. Almost at once a faint whistle damped by the snow 'Ock-acock-aooo'. We crowed back. We blew up, opened the regulator and crawled on.

'No block between here and Ely South' for the last time – and be thankful.

Soon we were at rest in the platform. Bob Aggas, large, relaxed, the first broad grin I had seen that day. Refreshment room, doors wide, waiting rooms bright with the tables covered with urns and cups and sandwiches. We took our turn at the tail of the queue. No one was saying to Bob: 'I am a friend of the Directors and I shall . . .' He had got his Public Relations well warmed up with tea.

When he had a minute Bob said to me:

'The North Continental went up at 8.30. He hasn't got to Bury yet.'

Arthur said hurriedly: 'We'll get home to March with our engine and Brake.'

'All right, Arthur.'

'On the way I'll be looking at Rules 178 and 179 and Block Regulation 25. See you soon.'

'See you soon.' With the threat about rules in mind I hoped not too soon.

LESSONS OF THE WINTER: II

Ely down platform; 11.30 a.m. January 1935; the snow whipping from the north east. We could feel it like shot pitting our faces.

'Into your office, Bob. One more call; to Bury. Let's hope the Continental's there. If not, see whether he can put his hand on the snow plough.'

But the Continental wasn't there and the plough had gone to Newmarket and then would be ploughing towards Ely; had left Bury at 9 p.m.

'He should not be far away, Bob.'

'Maybe'. Bob had been around long enough to be aware of committing himself to any optimism about running in snow.

'Which end is the Pilotman?'

'Your end.'

When the wires are down and we have no communication between signal boxes controlling a single line, the signalman cannot withdraw a token from the instrument to hand to the driver as an assurance that no train can be coming head on in the opposite direction. We therefore appoint a human token called a Pilotman. He authorises in person and by his presence the dispatch of each train.

This buttons up safety firmly. It is however important to have the Pilotman at the right end of the section to conduct the next train. That night he wouldn't be able, as once I did in fine weather, to ride a bike four miles to get himself to the right end.

So on that horrible night he was at least at the right end to bring the plough from Newmarket to Ely. Then we could set off to look for the Continental. I agreed with Bob what we should do and left him to the train load of passengers which he had either to get off to March and Peterborough or to doss down in Ely. Just the job for Bob.

I picked up my handlamp, went to the lamp room, topped it up with paraffin. (Once at night I topped up a lamp with petrol and caused a dramatic explosion on a footplate at Leicester Goods South.) I walked along the platform, down the ramp and set off along the line toward Ely Dock Junction where the line from Newmarket joins the Cambridge line. Not too bad with the wind over my left shoulder and the snow deep, maybe 8 inches by then, but not slippery. I climbed the steps, kicked my boots on the sill of the door to rid them of snow and went in.

'Any sign of the plough?'

'No sign of nothing.'

The signalman started to talk about floods which over the generation have covered the land round Ely more often and more importantly than snow.

'A couple of days heavy rain in the Midlands and forty-eight hours later it's here. Littleport and Hilgay, that's first and worst . . .'

And so on, back to Cromwell and the Bedford Level. The Box was warm. Ely Dock had a splendid chaise longue. I was full of tea and sandwiches. It was after midnight. I slept.

In a trice – which was in fact an hour – a hand was shaking my shoulder.

'It's here.'

I got up and looked out of the back window to the east. Two headlights were crawling down the little hill from the bridge over the Ouse. They stopped at the home signal. In a couple of minutes the Pilotman, the fireman and the Breakdown Foreman from Cambridge came in, a flurry of snow blew through the door.

'Seen the North Continental?'

'We passed him near Chippenham Junction; on our way to Newmarket.'

'He hasn't got to Bury. Was he moving?'

'Ay; he were a-going. If he isn't yet at Bury, he'll be in a drift in one of those cuttings round Kennet.'

'We'd best go look for him then, bor.'

No comment. They had been out ten hours; and would stick it for another twenty if they must. So, a light from the signalman to call the plough past the box and set back through the crossover. We went out and hoisted ourselves on to the footplate. This was a double-ended plough; in the middle the engine, a big six-coupled J20; at each end an old tender with its bows lengthened and sharpened with a high ram supported on each side by horizontal flanges. The whole enterprise weighed nearly two hundred tons. It could plough in either direction. It packed a lot of punch at 50 miles an hour. It carried in a caboose chains for towing trains out of drifts, ramps for rerailing wagons and jacks for rerailing itself. It carried a tea-urn and a heap of bread, butter and corned beef. Cosy. We set off confidently, the Pilotman being our guarantee that no train could be between us and Snailwell Junction. Ely Dock, Barway, Soham, Fordham and Snailwell told us that there was no block between . . . The snow falling was smaller and drier. It was driving almost horizontally, not only out of the sky but being flung, like spray from the head of a comber, from where it lay in the fields in great sheets across the line. As far as Chippenham Junction no problem. The gale blew it off the line as it blew it on. The rails still stood proud of the snow. The points at the signal boxes did not have to be moved. We went on merrily. We could see further. The side sheet in the cab kept the snow off us. The fire kept us warm. One of us had had a sleep. We were off on something real which might be a tale to tell in the mess rooms and shunters' huts down to our grandchildren. Our morale was high.

At Chippenham better still we found the guard of the Continental.

'We're in the cutting just past the bridge where the main road goes over the line' he said.

'Train all right? Engine alright for water?'

'Full diner service' he said; 'only 50 on the train. They're warm, kipping down, full of beer. Driver says he's all right till morning.'

We conferred; dead easy. On to the back of the train, chain on, pull back the mile to Chippenham, leave the train on one line, pass her on the other, plough the drift and all proceed orderly to Bury and, if need be, Ipswich in the morning.

The guard came with us. BANG – BANG – BANG – BANG – BANG over his fogs. Slowly now. We were within the walls of snow in the cutting. The bridge went smoothly overhead. The tail lamp of the Continental glowed. We stopped.

'I'll go through the train' said the guard. 'Snow's too thick by the sides. What shall I tell the driver?'

'We'll be chained on' said the Breakdown Foreman. 'Tell him to release his brakes and give us a crow when he's done so. Then we'll tow him out back on to the Down line between Chippenham and Snailwell.'

All hands out into the snow; haul the heavy chain out of the caboose; drawbar hook; and wait. Soon 'ock-aoodle-ooo.' We reply. The driver reverses. He open the regulator gingerly. We ease away until a light snatch tells us the chain is taut. Then he opens the regulator firmly. 'Ch . . . Ch . . . Chchchchchch.' We are slipping madly. He tries again. 'Ch . . . ch . . . chchchch;' A third time. Not a yard gained.

'We'll have to give her a pluck' he says. 'We shan't break anything. We may shake a few off their seats.'

He reverses, goes forward a yard or so. Into back gear again. Gives her steam. 'Ch . . . ch . . . ch . . . ch . . chchchchch.' It was a pluck all right.

'I think we got a yard' he said.

I was still standing in the cess. We had got a yard.

'One more and she'll come.'

So forward a yard; reverse again; 'Ch . . . ch . . . ch . . . chchch . . . ch . . . ch . . . ch . . .' and the train is moving gently past me. I wave my lamp to keep him going. Green light for slow but steady. As the train engine goes by I swing on to the step.

'And the top of the morning to you.' These are Ipswich men. They have come all the way out of lodge in Manchester.

'And who may you be?'

'I work around here' I said.

'And the best of British bloody luck to you. Wish I didn't,' he said. But there was a dining car carton on his ledge and there was tea in his can. The fireman was crooning something which presently came through as 'Join the NAVY and see the world. And woddidwe see? We saw the SEA!' So he wasn't amiss, if all he had on his mind was Ginger Rogers.

We stopped. The front end obviously conferring with the signalman at Chippenham. Restarted and a couple of train lengths further on stopped again. A whistle from the other end. The driver pulled his vacuum handle. A rush of air. The gauge dropped to zero. The fireman screwed on his handbrake. They would be there for maybe a couple of hours more, even if we had luck ploughing.

In a while the plough came through from Warren Hill, having run round the triangle. I got down and joined. Now it was our hour; what we were all about. We took a wrong line order from the signalman in case we didn't get through. We didn't want the Continental up our shirt, under some interpretation or other of the Time Interval System.

'No block between . . .' said Chippenham Junction sardonically. And we eased away; twelve miles to Bury and a lot of cutting. Visibility now maybe a hundred yards, if it was light which it wasn't. We would be ploughing blind at around fifty miles an hour. The rest of them on the footplate had done it all many times before. I was green. I was scared.

We stopped at Chippenham starter; got down; had a look round the leading plough, top bottom and sides. It all looked and felt pretty solid. We got back on the footplate. No need to shake the snow off. In seconds it ran off in streams. With the screens fitted a thermometer would register a heatwave.

Fore gear; 40 per cent; regulator open. CHARGE . . . hold on . . . rattle . . . clatter . . . bang (that's only the trailing axle box) . . . rattle . . . clatter . . . suddenly the air is full of heavy flying snow landing in the spectacles, the roof of the cab, the tender. No check and in twenty seconds we are through. We stop and look back; can't see a thing. Slowly we plough back through the cutting. No need. One line is clear with a high wall of snow on each side.

On gently to Kennet.

'Anything between us and Higham?'

'Only a lot of snow.'

'We'll take this wrong line order back to Chippenham. Come back and plough to Bury. We'll tell him to let the Continental come through to you.'

An hour later having repeated the procedure at Higham *and* having remembered to hold the catch points we are at Saxham.

'Anything between us and Bury?'

'You'll find the first cutting up to the eaves. Always a bad place.'

Fore gear; 40 per cent; CHARGE. We are in it. Top, bottom and sides. We are slowing . . . slipping . . . coming to a stand. Not a moment's delay. The Driver reverses. Opens the regulator. 'Ch . . . chchchch.' Not a yard. Sands open. Again 'Ch . . . chchchch.' Not a yard. We shall look clever if we have to be pulled out by the Continental and how many rules would Arthur find broken with that one?

The driver says: 'Get down and sand by hand, quick.' So we get buckets of sand out of the caboose, and scrapers for the rails. We treat under the engine and under the rear plough and ten yards behind. We stay on the floor, backs to the flying snow drifting hard into the cutting. But this time 'Chchch . . . ch . . . ch . . . ch . . .'

'Keep going' shouts the foreman. We hoist on to the step in turn.

Back for half a mile; reverse; sense of pawing the ground. CHARGE . The flying carpet of snow streams overhead. We are slowing . . . slowing . . . suddenly 'di-dah . . . di-dah . . .' accelerating again. We are through.

Back to Saxham to return the last wrong line order. The two low headlights of the Continental stand at his home signal. We clamber down for the last time to help his 'snowman' sweep the points of the crossover. We cross to the Down line. The Sandringham of the Continental clanks by. The fireman holds up both thumbs. The bright yellow windows of the coaches glide by faster. A hand or two clears a patch in a window. A face peers at us and is gone.

The fireman goes to the Box to carry on Rule 55 'remind the signalman of the presence of our train.' He sees the lever collar put on the Down Home Signal lever and comes back to us. The signalman allows the Continental twenty minutes for the three miles to Bury; then 'No block between here and Bury Yard. Proceed at caution.'

At Bury Stationmaster Wooltorton.

'The Parkeston's gone straight through. All clear to Ipswich. Their plough has been here and back.'

A thin light is filtering overhead. The station lamps can't disguise the dawn. It is getting on for eight o'clock. We have taken six hours from Ely. Daylight shews that the snow is easing. It is also infinitely chilly.

'Plough in the yard. Water, if the column isn't frozen.' Then off to the refreshment room. Eggs, bacon, scalding tea. Wonder when we shall get back to Cambridge.

A WINTER'S TALE: 1935

'Arthur' I said, 'keep that bloody door shut.' Notwithstanding, he went out on to the verandah of the brake, quested like a hound, hung over the rear partition, listened for several long moments, straightened up, turned, turned back again to the rear, listened and at long last came in and shut the door. This was for about the seventh time of asking in the twenty minutes we had been standing. He was like a cat on hot bricks and most unlike himself.

Every time he had done it the fog had wreathed out of the night through the door and vanished in the heat from the roaring stove. Outside all was white, thick and dripping from eaves, caps, eyebrows and nose. Inside we were snug. Why the fuss?

'Look' I said. 'We are on the main line. What are the chances of being run into from the rear? The signalmen have us On Line. The fogmen are out and will shoot any train behind us as it passes the distant at the box in the rear. The signalman will use his detonator placer if he runs past the home signal at danger. If he hasn't stopped by then the driver has to miss the starter and the advanced. Then he gets another detonator at our distant. Then he gropes toward the home that we're standing at and sees our tail lamp.'

This last was a mistake.

'At two yards range in this muck?' said Arthur. 'And *has* the signalman got us On Line? Suppose he's forgotten us. He'll have given Out of Section. He'll have accepted another, pulled off and the driver will be sailing towards us with all boards in his favour.'

'Rule 55' I said. 'Our fireman will be lying in the chaise longue in the Box, reminding the signalman of our presence.'

'Will he? Will he? It's in my bones there's something in the wind for us to-night.' And he made for the door for the eighth time.

However at that moment we moved. No warning. We were at Whittlesford Up Outer Home waiting to get in to the loop for examination; 41 equal to 49 of mixed coal and goods for

Temple Mills, Blackwall Yard; loose-coupled, but, standing on a raising gradient, the couplings were taut. The start was a smooth drag felt in the shoulders, and the stomach and the base of the spine. We came to a stand in the loop. Arthur got down, trudged to the telephone and rang the signalman to tell him that our train was inside the loop, complete and clear of the main line. We made our way forward. We met the tappers as they worked back from the front end. We walked back with them slowly; and gingerly, for the sleeper ends stood well proud of the ballast and were wet and slimy with years of spilled oil and with grease dripping from fat-boxes. All seemed in order. No hot boxes, no brake gear down, no buffer-locking. We put back one or two handbrakes which had come out of the notches and had dropped to chatter along as the brake blocks bounced on the tyres. As we neared the Brake the dim yellow stream of light of an express drew steadily by one the Up Main Line.

'That driver doesn't like it much to-night' said Arthur, 'not doing above 25.'

'Well, if we were in a car, we'd be at a dead stand, boy.'

But Arthur that night was not counting his blessings. He hove himself into the Brake in silence. In a while once again a smooth drag. The wheels of the Brake squealed harshly. Arthur released the wheel of the handbrake. We both went on to the verandah. As we passed the Box the window was open.

'Nothing behind you for a bit' shouted the signalman. 'You're right away Audley End.' He shut the window hurriedly. We saw him putting back levers. In a moment an express slid steadily past on the Down Line.

'6.36 London' said Arthur. 'About an hour late.'

We lumped along, lifting steadily out of the fens into the chalk hills of Essex. A rail joint about every four seconds, ten miles an hour or so. We would be a long time at that rate getting to the limit of the Cambridge District at Bishops Stortford, where I meant to leave Arthur and head for home.

Faintly from ahead we heard the crack of a detonator.

'Whittlesford said we would be right away Audley End' I commented.

'He did' said Arthur. 'Here it comes! We'll be out in this perishing night in a few minutes, rescuing something or other. You'll see.'

We stopped, drew ahead a few dozen yards and stopped again.

'Signalman telling the driver what to do. Us next' said Arthur.

Sure enough, the Brake drew up to the Box. 'Stop and Examine on the Down Line for the 6.36 London. Carriage door open. *Evening Standard* on the seat. Maybe someone's fallen out. Leave your brake on the main line. Put your train in the refuge. Unhook your engine. Pick up your brake. And go and examine the line. I've sent for the stationmaster. He'll ride on the engine. Both roads blocked till you clear them.'

Put like that it sounded easy. I had first to trudge up to the driver and get him to set the brake back clear of the points to the refuge; then walk back to meet Arthur trudging forward to tell me that he had unhooked the Brake; then trudge forward to tell the driver to draw ahead clear of the points; then walk back to meet Arthur for an assurance that he *was* clear and that the signalman had set them for the refuge; then trudge forward to tell the driver to set the train back in the refuge. Then I could ride back on the footplate and we were all within shouting distance for the two final moves. In all, forty minutes; and I at least was sweating in spite of the now near freezing fog.

'Pass the starter at danger' said the signalman 'examine the line. Report from Audley End.'

A long way, $1\frac{3}{4}$ miles from Great Chesterford to the auto signals at Littlebury; then another $2\frac{1}{4}$ miles to Audley End. Two tunnels on the way. Five men; stationmaster, whose responsibility it was; driver, fireman, guard and me hanging out looking and listening for an injured man reeling around in the fog or lying maimed or dead.

We set off at no more than five miles an hour. We could just see the cess on the far side of the down line. We should at least be able to examine the line and to deal with whatever we found.

'We shan't see him, if he's down a bank' said Arthur. 'Not that he's anywhere, I reckon. An evening paper on a seat's not much evidence. He'll have got out at Audley End and left it there. If it had been an umbrella on the rack, and a brief case that's different.'

Fair comment.

We lumbered on; bitterly cold; ears agonising; noses drip . . . drip . . . drip; eyes watering and straining at the far cess. The quiet beat of the exhaust and the slow thump of the wheels on the rail joints only emphasised the eternal distance which we still had to run. We dragged up to the auto at Littlebury, seen at green at maybe an engine-length. We stopped. The stationmaster 'phoned Audley End.

'Line examined between Chesterford and Littlebury. Nothing found.'

But whatever it was might be between Littlebury and Audley End. So after two minutes in the warm we went on. Suddenly the beat of the engine sharpened. The fog cleared. Audley End Tunnel. The exhaust mushroomed on the roof and rolled quickly down the arch and over our heads. In a couple of minutes we were through and out into the deep cutting beyond. Still nothing found. Through the second tunnel. The line widened into the two main lines and Up and Down loops. Harder to see across. Slower therefore. A few minutes later we slid clanking into Audley End Up platform. Stationmaster Duddell in attendance.

'Nothing found?'

'Nothing found. Both lines clear between Great Chesterford and Audley End. Resume normal working.'

Duddell looked at Arthur.

'Engine and Brake back to Cambridge for you' he said. 'Control say you'd take another hour to dig your train out of Chesterford and your enginemen have been on six hours now.'

'And what about me?' said Arthur. 'Haven't I been with them, bearing the heat and burden of the day?' said that master of inapt metaphor. But it suited me.

We set off through the crossover propelling the Brake with a white light on its bracket. Arthur felt better about being run into when he had 150 tons of engine behind him. Nor was he much bothered about being pushed into anything in front, the last train having gone down over two hours before.

On the way home he said:

'You examine the line like that with an engine, don't you?'

'Regulation 14A' I said.

'Where does it tell us to take a Brake?'

I thought.

'It's not in 14A. I don't know. It's sense, if you may find a passenger lying around.'

'It is in the Appendix. You've got the reason right.'

'Then why didn't we take a stretcher?'

'We did.'

'How come?'

'Two shunting poles through the arms and pockets of an overcoat' – he paused – 'Probably yours.'

THE VACUUM: I

A-many years ago there were two types of brake. The Great Western, the Great Northern and the Euston Confederacy used the Vacuum – the Great Western, different as usual from the rest, required 24 inches on the gauge; the rest 21. The Westinghouse compressed air brake was the practice on the Great Eastern and on some minor companies like the North Eastern and some nameless lines in Scotland, not to mention the Brighton and Isle of Wight lines in the south. Liverpool Street and stations east and north were always energetic with the cough-pant-cough of the Westinghouse pumps. Each type had its protagonists. 'We know beyond peradventure' said the vacuum boys, 'when we have got a brake throughout the train because we can't start it unless we have.' And in general they were right. Often they couldn't start it when they did have one. Ask the Leicester or Darnall enginemen how often they tried to start out of Banbury with 21 inches on the engine and 24 inches on the train, as left by the Great Western men who had brought it in; and how long it took to go back and pull all the strings, release all the brakes, and begin to create the brake all over again. But enginemen had to be new to the Great Western game to fall for that one. A second time the train would be ready with only the handbrakes applied when they backed on with their engine. Then the guard would forget to take the handbrake off in the front brake and there would be a lovely flat wheel by the time he stopped at Woodford.

'Nevertheless' said the vacuum boys, 'we are safer. With the Westo you can have the cocks shut between engine and train. You can start and sail along with a brake only on the engine. And when you want to stop you land up in Smith's bookstall.' 'Granted' said the Swedies, 'we could run our railway like that, even if we don't; what we can't do is to work our sharp jazz service, let alone the Ilfords and Gidea Parks with the vacuum. Too slow to stop. Too long to blow the brake off.' And of course a lot of other argument too. So the Westinghouse Company went on making Westo brakes for the Westo and Vacuum brakes for the rest. And all were happy until the amalgamation of 1923 when in the sacred name of standardisation the LNER among others decided to adopt the vacuum brake. The North Eastern and the rest complied. The Swedie said 'We can't and won't.' This was out of character because often the Swedie, when ordered to adopt a standard practice, adopted it. Once a Chief Operating Superintendent visited Liverpool Street and found that the signalmen were not ringing one bell 'Call attention' before every bell signal. Bill Crow rang one bell at Assistant Superintendent Jimmy Sharpe and ordered that the new standard Block Regulations should be carried out. Next day the signalmen carried them out to the ultimate Hogsnorton. By 8.30am the peak was running forty minutes late for that reason alone. And that was the end of that. The Swedies however, did not even try the vacuum on their inner suburban services; and of course when we electrified the air brake became standard, not only for the inner but for outer also.

However, the rest of the passenger service turned to the vacuum. And as wagons began to be fitted with the

Freight on the Great Eastern section of the LNER was often in the hands of these small Class J15 0–6–0s which could be seen all over East Anglia. (*L&GRP/ David & Charles*)

continuous brake and as Swedie engines were converted, so did the freight. When I went to Whitemoor as Assistant Yardmaster there were two 'vacuums'. The Down Vacuum and the Up Vacuum. 9.30pm Spitalfields to Whitemoor, splitting there into the 12.15am to Pyewipe and 12.30am to Doncaster. 9.38pm Ardsley Up, detaching and attaching on the Main Line at Whitemoor and running on to Spitalfields. These trains were worked generally by March enginemen with Gresley K3s or J39s and by Whitemoor guards. And Westo to a man, we were all pretty green at the Vacuum.

We had two receptions, 'The Dirt Track,' in the little Norwood Yard, and fourteen sidings of which three served the tranship-shed. From 10pm onwards we would shunt the 7.15pm Ipswich, the 7.30 Norwich, the Cambridge, the Lynn, the Lowestoft. We would knock out all the unfitted wagons for the later slow mop-up services. We would knock out the Colwicks and the Spaldings, the Down pick-ups, the Up Roads and the Tranships. We would have a road of Pyewipe fitted for Lincoln, Sheffield, Manchester and Liverpool; and another of Doncaster fitted for the West Riding, Teesside, Newcastle and Scotland. Not very good railway work for an amalgamated company and in a few years we were doing it very differently, making through trains to Manchester, Stockton, Newcastle and Niddrie. But in 1933 this is how it was.

Around 10.15 Control would ring: 'Down Vacuum 47 on. 17 Whitemoor, 13 Pyewipe, 17 Doncaster. Looks like being right time'. OK. So we could attach equal to 37 of our own Pyewipes to the 12.15; and 33 to the 12.30 Doncaster. Note that the Ipswich, Norwich and Lynn wagons had become 'ours'. And in giving a good service yards have to think of them as such. The guards, on duty an hour early for the Vacuums, would go down their wagons and in the intervals of the shunting would nip between the wagons, slip on the screw coupling, take an end of each vacuum hose in each hand and with a turn of the wrist bring the faces together with the washers not twisted, and with the lugs engaged (we hoped). Sometimes one would find a cripple. 'Rocher's been down and red carded one'. And the pilot would have to knock it out when he had a chance. But on the whole the examiners did their job on the Dirt Track and only red-carded in the sidings the very occasional one which we had damaged in shunting.

Some guards, still apprehensive of the speed of the vacuums, would try to get Green Cards 'Fit to travel to destination.' Then for repair, knocked out. And you had to know your men. Arthur Helstrip, waxed moustache, *point de vice* but no nonsense. Arthur Brewster, would chance anything and came to a bad end. Arthur Robinson, clean collar, freshly shaven, bit of a sea lawyer, watch him for delays. Fred Charles, the foulest mouthed man for a hundred miles. Occasionally Whitemoor guards had a passenger turn. So Fred, fearing no evil in his best uniform on No 7 at Liverpool Street to take the 4.15pm to Peterborough, performing with old-world courtesy. 'Good afternoon madam' to a little old lady in black. 'Good afternoon Guard.' Not to be outdone. 'Does this train stop at the Green?' 'Which

Green would that be, Madam?' 'Bethnal Green' – followed by an Anglo-Saxon expletive. But Fred didn't learn about language from her. He knew it all before. Not so much, however, about the vacuum brake. Jack Neave, who knew it all and let everyone know he knew it all. He didn't endear himself to the drivers. Slogger Godfrey . . .

About 11.30 we would be shunted up. Class I shunter Tommy Woodbine, if it were he, would lean on the shunting pole outside the ground frame where Hodge Jackman had been slamming points to his orders. The chasers, Dick Green and Jack Talbot would congregate in the frame. In a few minutes two lights in a row would slide quietly along the Dirt Track. A couple of us would go down with the examiner. Another on the Pilot. One would unhook the engine and send him up the engine line to await his ticket from the guard. The rest would start pulling strings on the wagons to release the brakes. The examiner would tap wheels, feel axle boxes with the back of his hand and peer at the brake gear and buffer castings. Not unknown for a couple of wagons to arrive buffer-locked, having travelled who-knows-how-far like that. Always fun unlocking them by placing them on a sharp curve just so and easing away; or if locked vertically, with a loose coupling and a jerk and hope we're not off the road as a result. If we are, ramps and packing quick and with luck a pull and a bump and in ten minutes we're on again and no one the wiser – provided Rocher says the wagons can go. He prefers it that way. For if not he has to go down on his knees and undo the buffer, draw it out, put it back and do it up again. Always good to get your incentives in the right place.

By this time we have met the guard. He has confirmed the details of the load and told us of any trouble. Pilot on. A light from the rear 'Go ahead'. Up over the knuckle; reverse. Come back slow. Tommy unscrews and slips three couplings. The brake van slides into No 5. The Doncasters roll smoothly onto No 3; the Pyewipes on to No 11; the Whitemoors on to No 9, the middle road of the shed. The Pilot slides back out of the way toward the Dirt Track. Hodge opens the points from the engine line. Tommy waves a lamp, once and then again.

And the two K3s clank slowly back on to No 11 and No 3. With luck the whole train has rolled together as it was shunted so that the guard has got brake and wagons coupled, screwed and piped up. Some wouldn't. So stand by to get your own hands dirty – as if they weren't as black as your boots already. 'Forty-five equal to forty-eight on, Driver'. A white light from the rear up and down 'Blow up'. The driver turns on the big ejector. Gradually as you peer into the cab the needle creeps round toward the standard 21 inches or the minimum for freight, 17.

If you are lucky – and you have maybe ten or twelve minutes before 12.15 to be lucky in – the next sign is a green light from the brake van. The Inspector shews a green to the frame. The frame responds. The driver whistles briefly. He shuts the large ejector and opens the small. He opens the regulator gingerly. The exhaust is light and slow as he collects his train and walks her up the gradient to the knuckle. The wagon wheels ring high and sweet round the outlet from the sidings. The brake van sways towards you. The guard is leaning out ready to say something to Tommy and then to exchange hand signals with the fireman as soon as he is out of the yard. You think you have done enough.

THE VACUUM: II

'Stand back, Arthur, I'm coming aboard'. Hand lamp in left hand, two quick strides, left hand on rail, right foot on lower step, swing, right hand on rear rail. . . . Arthur nudges the cross bar out, up the two other steps and I slip past him on to the rear verandah. He replaces the cross bar, calls to Tommy 'Booking right time'. We are in fact seven minutes early but he may 'want the time' to cover some misdemeanour of his own or of the driver's on the run. He waves his lamp, white light, slowly from side to side as we swing right handed through the connection yard to Main. An answering light comes from the fireman. The brake van surges forward with a smooth drag as the driver, knowing the train is complete, squares his shoulders and sets himself to speed up to sixty.

The small red spot of the fire in the ground frame vanishes. The yellow pools of light in the yard and the hooded shapes of the Red Vans dwindle. The brilliance of the floodlights in the Down Hump Yard go steadily by. And we are left to a high riding moon, the square ploughlands and straight wide drains of the fen. I go inside and shut the door. Arthur is in the right hand seat. I take a quick look around. The fire in the stove is bright. The leading door is not stuffed with paper round the edges – so it fits; no draughts. There is no padding in the sockets of the side lights so the brake is not a rough rider. Except for our hand lamps in their wooden holders in the floor, no light. All is warm and shut off from the world with the familiar comforting chatter of brake-blocks and the thump of the rail joints – di . . . dah, di . . . dah. A long wheelbase Queen Mary has a slow double thump, not the fussy quadruple ti-ti-ti-tum of a passenger coach.

I settle in the left hand seat. Right leg propped on the column of the hand brake; head resting on the rear cushion. The smooth drag out of the yard has assured me that there are no loose couplings. We shall not get a sudden pluck and our heads cracked against the cushions. Now, if the guard had been Jack Neave, I would have been on the look out. A driver would give Jack a fourpenny one now and again to set him up for something Jack had said to him earlier. Arthur was filling in his journal with the details of the start of the journey. Train, load, engine, number, driver's name, time. He would follow with the driver's ticket which he would hand to the driver at Pyewipe. Professionally he paused for a minute and in that minute we hammered over the right angled crossing at Murrow, where the Midland & Great Northern crosses the GN and GE Joint Line. Then he finished the job.

By this time we were well into the swing. Looking through the forward glass of the ducket the green eye of each signal hurried toward me and flipped by. The smooth rush through platforms came often and seemed to magnify the speed.

'Must be pretty rough up front on that old K3,' Arthur shouted.

I grunted loudly. Talking in a brake van at speed is no fun

for anybody. We sat lapped in a warm and companionable silence, watching the line of vans ahead snaking gently from side to side, listening for any untoward noise. At Cowbit the noise sharpened as we roared past a train of coal empties put aside for us in the down loop; probably the 10.40pm Whitemoor to Colwick. Must have been late starting or he would have been beyond Sleaford and off on the Nottingham line before we were near him. Spalding, and the close headway distants were all off for us. The station was in darkness. Yard lights and drifts of steam from the pilots glimpsed and were gone. A moment's unsteadiness over the facing junction to the East Lincolnshire line and again we were tearing through the fen with the signals and stations hurrying smoothly past. In the moonlight the streamer of steam from the engine looked silver, lit every so often to gold as the fireman opened the firehole door. Life was cosy and eternal.

Arthur sat up straight. He turned his head, questing like a hound with his nose.

'Hot box' he shouted.

'I don't get it' I roared back. Nor did I. Nor do I often, having a sense of smell which in the war was the despair of the authorities. What was the future of Britain if the District ARP officer could not distinguish mustard gas from phosgene? We went out on the rear verandah. We each peered forward at the shouldering vans. Nothing to be seen.

'It's there somewhere, sure enough' said Arthur. 'But it's not a flamer so it's OK for a while. Not at Sleaford yet. We shan't get to Pyewipe without having to stop.'

Arthur had, of course, control of the situation. In general the driver or fireman will not recognise a hot box in stage I. The smell does not travel forward. A signalman may (should) see or smell it and get the signalman ahead to stop the train by sending seven bells 'Stop and examine'. The guard on a partly-fitted or loose-coupled train should carry out that splendid rule 148(c) which tells him to apply his hand-brake sharply and release it several times, so that he sort of plucks at the driver's skirt. The driver looks back, sees the guard waving a red hand lamp at him and brings the train to rest or, and this does not appear in BR's rules, the Guard may – and probably does – take off his tail lamp as he passes a signalbox. The signalman recognising an emergency which is not immediate and does not affect the other line, sends forward 'stop and examine'. And all is squared up safely and with the minimum of disturbance to trains on the opposite or adjacent lines. In this case being in charge of the Vacuum, Arthur could pull the tap of his brake and arrest the proceedings.

This he was in no hurry to do. His professional judgement was to go on. If by chance we could get to Pyewipe, the goods could be transhipped into another wagon in the yard within an hour or two. Maybe their delivery would be almost as planned. If we stopped short, an empty wagon would have to come down on the morning pick-up. Maybe extra staff would have to be sent from Sleaford or Lincoln to help with the handling. And some train would have to be stopped out of course to pick up the freshly loaded wagon. Delay, cost, fuss. We were not in any danger. So let us go on.

We swung into the avoiding line round Sleaford; but soon a bright star appeared low on my side of the train, about twenty wagons ahead. And sure enough the next signal but one which hurried toward me had a yellow eye. The brakes went smoothly on. We came down from our sixty to maybe fifteen and swung left-handed into Blankney loop; and came to rest. Arthur screwed on his handbrake. No need to reverse a side-light. We didn't carry them. We were the Vacuum. We got down on the cess side and walked forward. Near the offending wagon we met the fireman.

'Bobbie says Stop and Examine for a hot box. Unhook and when the Doncaster vacuum's by, draw ahead and put it in the yard.'

Arthur took the details of the wagon for his journal. 'NE 743121 Parkeston Quay to Manchester, Deansgate. Perishable. Butter.' He went between the wagons, parted the vacuum pipes. He put the leading one on the dummy plug so that the driver could create a brake. He undid a few turns of the coupling and slipped it off the hook. We walked forward to the signalbox. Arthur got the signalman's permission to use the control phone. He passed the details.

'What, how much butter? Well if that wagon run hot, she's got a load. Butter's heavy stuff – eight or ten tons I'd say.'

A bell rang sharply: once, acknowledged, then twice 'Train on Line'. The signalman moved his peg accordingly. With his left hand he rang his bell forward; one pause, three, pause one. 'No 1 Express Goods' Acknowledged. The forward block indicator flicked to line clear'. He pulled his levers; advanced starter, starter, inner home, outer home, distant. Three minutes and over the roofs of our train a drift of hurrying steam. Then two lights on a buffer beam lurching and clattering by. A glimpse of the cab with driver and fireman seated and holding on. The long train chattering. The red-eye of the tail lamp dwindling in the distance. In the box movement of levers. The signalman waves a white light. A short whistle and our engine draws ahead with the front section, past the box, over the connection to the yard. Frosty now. The roofs of the vans sparkle, silver and purple and blue. The sleepers are covered in a white slippery rime. Arthur and I pick our way gingerly. He calls the driver back into the yard. He uncouples the wagon, puts the hose on the dummy plug of the wagon ahead. Meantime I have been pinning down the hand brake on each side of the wagon detached. A handlamp waved at the box, response, draw ahead again over the crossing, back on our train. I ride on the engine. Arthur goes up into the box to sign the Train Register, Rule 55. I couple up. The signal comes off. The driver takes the train slowly by for me and then Arthur to get aboard. And in half an hour we are in Pyewipe. 25 late records Arthur.

We have nearly an hour before we take our back working, the Up Vacuum. We walk over to the mess room. We settle. Arthur shares his 'snap' with me for I haven't brought anything.

'When you were passing me in rules the other day' he began 'you were wrong about . . .' And so we settled to the traditional, unending and absorbing railwaymen's argument about rules. He had been waiting for his chance for about four weeks I suppose. It must have been frustrating for him that the noise in the brake van made it impossible earlier to get it off his chest.

2.15pm WHITEMOOR TO STRATFORD LOCO

Arthur was in dispute with departure foreman Ben Mitchell.

'I won't take it' I heard him say as I walked across the path from the yardmaster's office to the departure cabin.

'It's that brake or nothing, Arthur.'

'Why can't I have that Queen Mary?'

'I've told you before.' Ben is very large with a great slab of a face and a grin like a double crease in the seat of your pants. 'That Queen Mary is for the 1.50 Norwich, Class A and we can't put Swedies on them.'

'So I've got the Swedie 20 tonner?'

'That's right, Arthur. There's just the Queen Mary and the Swedie on the Brake Kip.'

'Why can't the Pilot go down 26 and bring up some more?'

Ben sighed. 'The West Side Pilot is drawing the shed. The East Side is making up the 2.50 pick-up. And the Middle Pilot doesn't come out till 5.'

'So, may I go down with my train engine when he comes . . .'

'All right, Arthur. If you're late you'll have to take the delay.'

At the talk of delay I got ready to intervene; but Arthur picked up his traps and walked across to the inclined plane of the brake kip. On one road stood the Queen Mary; on the other the Great Eastern 20 tonner. It looked like an ancient garden shed, garnished with a few hand-rails and plonked on top of four wheels. He came back carrying a shunting pole, still muttering and making the most of it. 'One sidelight missing, no sprags, no tow rope.'

'In the lamp-room' said Ben. 'Sprags lying here. What the hell will you do with a towrope working a block load of Stratford loco coal?'

'The rule says that a Guard must have in his Brake Van. . . .

Mr Fiennes examined me in rules the other day.' I had indeed, but the rule didn't come up. I kept mum.

Ben's creases broadened. He said no more. And in a few seconds Arthur took himself to the lamp room. When he came out carrying the holder of a side light and wiping his fingers delicately on some waste I said: 'I've been early turn to-day – nearly finished. I'll come with you some of the way.'

I picked up two sprags. We walked to his brake van and put them through the door.

Then down to No 20. Stratford Loco was mostly in big wagons, red 20 tonners vacuum fitted or piped and labelled 'Return to Warsop'. Pronounce it high at the back of the mouth, short and softly: 'Wahsup'. Good, big, hard steam coal, fit for Clauds and 1500s to be thrashed on to Norwich and Lowestoft and Clacton and Parkeston and Southend. The wagons stood in cuts of six or eight as they had been loaded together. Arthur slipped on five or six couplings and then uncoupled in the final place. We ducked through to the other side – irregularly, but no train was being shunted at the hump end – and walked back toward the Departure, looking at the wagons for correct labelling and for defects.

When we got to the head of our train our engine stood in the engine line. At our signal Ben called him back. Arthur used the engine coupling – rightly, as it then was. The fireman took the tail lamp off the engine and put a lamp on the right hand buffer beam, Class C.

'34 on, equal to 65, Driver', said Arthur. The engine was a Gresley O2, one of the big boys, Class 8 and the maximum for the line.

'Draw ahead into the Departure line when you get the tip from the cabin and stop for us to run the brake on.'

Arthur held his right arm out shoulder high to Ben. Response. The engine coughed into its snifting valve and began to move. We walked across to the brake van, clambered aboard. We stowed the sprags. Arthur put the sidelamp in place. As our train came to a stand in the Departure line he released the wheel of the hand brake and we ran gently down the kip and on to the rear of the train. The departure shunter

The control tower of Whitemoor marshalling yard just north of March. It was one of the most modern yards on the LNER in the 1930s.

coupled us on. Arthur got patiently down, unhooked the wagon coupling, coupled the screw coupling of the brake van and screwed it up tight. He got aboard. He went to the left side and held out his arm to the driver. A whistle and we moved toward the outlet signal at Whitemoor Junction. Ben made a rude gesture in our general direction.

The outlet signal came off. We ground slowly over the junction with the Wisbech line and into the avoiding line behind March station. We kept going. March East, unusually, had his crossing gates open for us. Out Main Line there. The directing distant at March South was off for the St Ives Loop. We swung right handed into the fen; past Wimblington, past Chatteris where, because this was August, they were loading up to eighty wagons a day of carrots in Hyfits for all over England and Scotland; up Somersham bank, dragging slow but steady, and down the other side.

Then I knew why Arthur didn't want that Swedie brake. All brakes chatter amiably and thump. Some hunt. Swedies at any high speed bang and throw themselves backwards and forwards and sideways in a frenzy. We hung on grimly. Arthur's journals and notebook made their way across the seat and flopped unheard in the din to the floor. In due course we ran out on to the level. Speed dropped to 20mph. Swedie settled down to bang along on a fairly straight and even keel. We rubbed a few bruises.

'I'll get her red carded at Whittlesford, I will.' said Arthur. If it had been Fred Charles, the vocabulary would have been graphic, with four-letter words, but Arthur is a gentleman. And I was sorry to think that I was going to be with him only for the riding uphill. He would have twenty-five miles from Bishops Stortford to Temple Mills mostly downhill and, if he got the distants off, mostly at a speed which would haul the Swedie into a paroxysm of shudders and judders and bounces and lashings of her tail. And of course a guard is in charge of his train. He is the judge of what is safe. If he said to the examiner at Whittlesford: 'This brake is unsafe' it would be a foolhardy examiner who failed to put on it a red card 'Not to Go.'

We were not getting distant signals against us. Most of the stations on the St Ives loop had level crossings. Most of the signalmen at most of the stations gave preference to road traffic over coal trains. Most of the coal trains were therefore late, missed their path at Chesterton Junction and found themselves 'in the cupboard' at Trumpington, just beyond Cambridge, for passenger trains or express freights to pass. Most of the train crews did not openly object to the overtime so earned. So, up the cupboard and expecting to be there for half-an-hour.

'Why do we have to use the engine coupling? Its usually a screw-coupling. Its heavier than the three-link. We have to unscrew it to get it on and screw it up again.'

Guards, of course, and Arthur was no exception in most aspects of guarding, do the easy thing – except when it suits. So I said:

'Apart from to-day, the last time you had a screw-coupled brake, did you use the wagon coupling or the other?'

'The brake coupling, of course.'

'Why? It's a screw.'

'So you can screw it up tight to the wagon ahead and get a smoother ride – 'course.'

'OK. So there's some sense in the other too. When I was in the Manchester District we had a train in Hadfield loop. When he got the board he couldn't start – train too heavy. So he set back on the brake van to get the couplings loose. Then he reversed and opened the regulator. He shot ahead – light engine. The wagon coupling had slipped off the drawbar hook on the tender.'

'So', said Arthur, 'if he had used the engine coupling, the coupling might have slipped between the second and third, or the third and fourth . . . or any of them.'

'So it might. Rules don't make railways safe; only a bit safer than they were. Anyway in the Manchester case when he set back on the brake van the brake didn't hold and the whole train ran back the loop into the sand drag.'

'What happened to the guard?'

'It woke him.'

Arthur looked at me very severely. He is *for* the grade of guard. My comment was a denigration.

'Anyway', he said, 'It's not in Rules to use the engine coupling,' and he produced his Rule Book. He left me to look, which is why I didn't hear the train start. On a loose coupled train, when the driver opens the regulator, clinks on a rising and accelerating note as the coupling pull taut in turn. Clank . . . clank . . . clank . . . clank . . . clink . . . clink . . . clink . . . clink . . . clonk. The final clonk is your head cracking up against the ducket, which happens if you are not attending; which I wasn't, being deep in the absence of what I wanted to find in the Rule Book.

Arthur was sympathetic and partly mollified. 'It's in the Appendix' he said. We trundled on following the 2.40 Hunstanton. We were now half an hour late and would be in Whittlesford for the 5.30 Cambridge stopping train. If Arthur didn't get the examiner to red-card the Brake we would be 55 minutes late away. Well, Arthur would be. For me, if I didn't wait to see what happened I would catch the 4.15 London and be in March at 7.12. Tea, a quick trip to the Royal Exchange for a pint of the best Old south of Burton and an early bed before 6am on in the morning.

About noon I was on the Down Hump on my Lawful Occasions when the 6.40am Temple Mills ran in. In due course the guard made his way toward us – Arthur.

'Well?' I said.

'We were three hours late at the Mills' said Arthur. 'The examiner red-carded the brake.'

'Arthur!' I said.

'Oh,' he said, 'not for rough-riding. Hot-box. I didn't tell you at the time. Didn't want to rake up again your lousy sense of smell.'

TOW-ROPE

'You remember' said Arthur, 'coming with me not long ago on the 2.15 with a Swedie Brake?'

I did. Arthur had made a lot of a fuss about taking it at all; and indeed had got only half way when the examiner at Whittlesford had crippled it for a hot box.

'Well', he said, cocking an eye; 'You may remember that I mentioned the word 'Tow-rope'.'

Again I did. He had not refused in terms to take that Brake without a tow-rope; indeed he could not have done so because they were not required equipment. But he had, so to speak, tossed the word lightly in the air and hoped. However, it had fallen on stony ground, the ears of Ben Mitchell. And no more had been heard of it. I was sorry because that Brake was a stinker. Indeed all Swedie Brakes should have been grounded but in 1933 in the depression we were short of Brakes and short of money to build better; so, as often on the LNER we were making do.

I said: 'Towing only where authorised; then only on adjacent roads when no other train is approaching; and a lot of other dum-dum-dum. They seem to be frightened of it. Funny it doesn't say, like fly-shunting, only to be done by experienced men.'

I had been looking it up.

Arthur said: 'Did you hear about Stephen and the Tow-rope?'

I hadn't but it was likely to be good. There were stories about Stephen. Red, burly, sweating like a bull, usually in his shirt sleeves in winter, tearing into it without the least thought where he was going. Train engine off the Receptions – shunt the train – engine off the Receptions – shunt the train – engine off the Receptions – shunt the train – engine off the Receptions ... 'Stephen', roared Yardmaster Stone once, looking at seven engines on the engine line, 'If you want to assemble March Loco Depot here, just tell me and we'll send for the Depot Master to take charge.' He was a hard working head shunter, always looking at his boots. He had been out as a guard, maybe five years.

'Well ...' said Arthur, 'I was on late turn for the Fruit Working and being still single, we were collaborating on the 8.40am Whitemoor to Spalding Pick-up. And on a Pick-up you have plenty of time for gossip. You arrive at Guyhirne, place the empty vans for the fruit in the siding, take the road van into the shed, help to unload what is theirs, draw out and go on to Murrow. There you put the whole train aside, go through similar procedures and settle down while the Passenger and a few empty trains warble by. Then the signalman may find you a gap to slip you on to French Drove to do it again and so to Postland and so to Cowbit. It is not much use being in a hurry. If you get on to Control, one turn will say 'Stay where you are for the Passenger and three.' The others will make it either two or four. All three turns will think you odd to be in a hurry with a Pick-up.

'A Pick-up is after all the Old Man's Home. When you are medically or domestically past holding on to Swedie Brakes with teeth and claws or lodging in hostels or private lodges far from home, then a benevolent yardmaster will talk his staff representative into putting you into the Old Man's Gang.

This means that you go back to the young man's job of having some shunting to do. But it doesn't come very hard; and you do it nice and leisurely, if you have to do it at all. Charlie Bunting regularly had the 7.10am Whitemoor to Lincoln. We used to make up his train, couple it, light the fire, see that he had his sidelights, tail lamp, shunting pole and sprags. When he arrived we used to put in his hand a list of the train and where each wagon would be detached. We headed up his journal. We counted the detonators in his bag, saw that he had his flags and that his lamp had a wick, some oil and red and green shades. We added to his sandwiches and tea if he looked short. Then we led him to his brake van, loaded him in, coupled on his engine and gave right away. All Charlie had to do at Whitemoor was to release his hand brake.

Then we telephoned Postland: '7.10am Whitemoor, Charlie Bunting; Road Van, 6 Fitted Empty for you, 3 coal, 1 cattle food,' and the goods porter at Postland would receive Charlie, do his shunting for him, put a new list of his train in his hand, give right away to the driver and telephone Cowbit. '7.10am Whitemoor, Charlie Bunting. . .' Charles went along happily for years and came to no harm.

So, plenty of time, when Arthur said: 'Stephen was working the Shippea Hill Beet. Have you ever been to Duck Drove?'

'Only a footnote in the time table to me.'

'Well, Duck Drove is a siding on the Down side between Padnal and Shippea Hill. Not much doing now except in the Beet season. You get the key from Padnal Box. Go forward with your train and stop short of the connection to the siding. You get down, walk to the ground-frame, unlock it and put the distant and home signals to danger. Then you can hook off your engine, pick up what's in the siding, put the empties in if you've brought any, back on to your train, pull the signals off again, lock the frame and go on to Shippea Hill.'

'Which' I said, 'gets the key at the wrong end. It's wanted for next time at Padnal.'

'So' said Arthur, who is a great one for the word 'so', which means 'we've thought of that already'.

'So' said Arthur, 'the key goes back to Padnal on the next

train, which may be yours when you have shunted Shippea Hill; or the porter may take it on his bike. 'But on this particular day there was a relief signalman on duty at Padnal. And he had had an idea. He said to Stephen: 'What's the load for your engine?'

'37 of mineral'. He'd got a little old Black Goods, a J15.

'So that's, say, 31 or 32 actual wagons, there being a lot of 12 tonners. OK. Well, I've 25 Ely's here now and there's probably a dozen at Duck Drove. So you'd best do a trip to Ely sugar factory before going to Shippea Hill. Drop down to Duck Drove and bring them back facing road on the Down line. I'll give you a wrong line order.'

'How will I run round them?' said Stephen. 'There's no crossover; just the plain lead from the siding to the Down Main.'

'Ah' said Bobbie; 'I've found a Tow-Rope.' Stephen went on making difficulties.

'I've towed at Pymoor siding by Stonea – same sort of working, ground frame and signals. Can we tow at Duck's Drove?'

'Blessed if I know, mate. There's no Supplement to the Appendix in this box.'

'I haven't got one' said Stephen. 'We'll have a go!'

So the Bobbie made out the wrong line order, signalman to driver; 'I authorise you to travel on the Down Line in the wrong direction from Duck Drove siding to this signal box.' And told Stephen where to find the Tow-Rope.

Stephen's plan when he got to Duck Drove was to go through the rigmarole of unlocking the frame and putting the signals to danger. He would then draw ahead over the points and knock his Brake Van on top of the loaded wagons so:

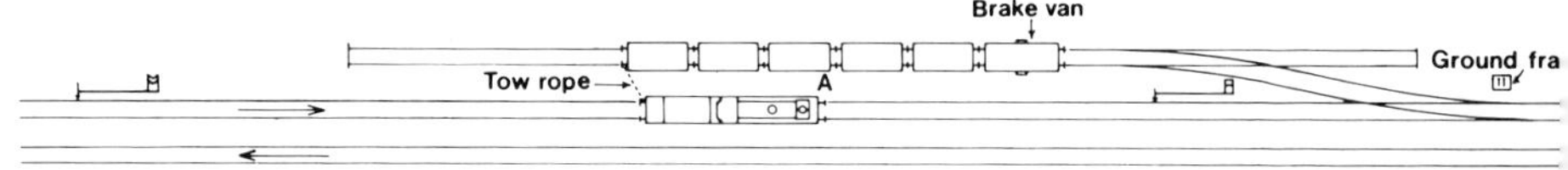

He would then bring his engine to point A and attach the rearmost wagon to it with the tow-rope. The driver would, at the word of command, set off rapidly for ten wagon lengths toward Norwich, thereby accelerating the Brake Van and wagons out on to the Main Line. The engine would stop short of the home signal. The train could come to rest. The engine would back on. Stephen would couple up. And the whole would return facing road to Padnal under the protection of the Wrong Line Order. That was the plan.

'Stephen carried three quarters of it out to perfection' recounted Arthur. 'He opened the frame, set back into the siding with the Brake, closed the wagons together, coupled them up and on to the Brake. He loaded the Tow-Rope on to the engine, came out of the siding, shut the points and set back to point A. So far, so very good.'

By this time I was hugging myself with glee in the sure and certain knowledge of what would befall poor looking-at-his-boots Stephen.

'Stephen' said Arthur, 'attached one end of the Tow rope to the tender. He took the other across to the last wagon, which happened to be a seven-plank Southern high-side. He couldn't find any towing lugs, so he debated to himself not whether to abandon the whole scheme and go on to Shippea Hill, which he could have done with only two shunting moves – Brake back to Down Main Line; wagons out and on to it and square the wrong line order somehow; but whether he should attach the tow-rope to the hornplate or to the drawbar hook of the wagon. He chose the drawbar hook. And gave the driver a fierce wave of the arm to go ahead.

'The little old Black Goods started with a bang. In a minute Stephen was running hard to keep up, so as to nip the tow-rope off the drawbar hook as soon as they had got enough speed. He tripped over a pile of beet lying in the four-foot an fell flat on his face. The driver couldn't see what had happened till too late. The wagons trundled inexorably on. The tow-rope was taut between engine and wagons. The whole enterprise arrived at the home signal; engine on the Down Main; wagons in the sidings; the home signal between the two. First the iron ladder buckled and caved in toward the post; then the post itself swayed, made to recover and fell athwart the line of wagons which was half way out on to the Main Line. Four derailed; beet everywhere; both Main Lines blocked.'

Arthur paused for effect. He can tell a tale.

'If I was examining you in Rules' he asked, 'what would you say was wrong with that lot?'

'Stephen' I said.

3

The Second World War

GRANTON DOCK

It is, maybe, the essence of farce that some event takes place during which someone does some wrong thing, and thereafter with entire logic and everyone concerned carrying out their part with the utmost dedication the whole affair comes to a hilarious end. So it was in the autumn of 1939 when a locomotive, thirty-seven wagons and a brake van ended up beneath the waters of Granton Dock.

It all began in Haymarket Tunnel just west of Edinburgh Waverley Station. A freight train, partly fitted with the vacuum brake, had come to a stand with 'vacuum failure'. The driver tried to re-create his brake power by using his big ejector. No useful result. So he said to his fireman: 'Go back, Charlie. There must be a leak somewhere. Twisted washer maybe. You'll hear it. Put it right and come back.' So off went Charlie listening for the hiss of indrawn air and shining his handlamp on the pipes between the wagons to see what was amiss.

After a while he came back to the engine and said to the driver: 'Nothing to be heard or seen; shall I pull the cords and we go forward unfitted?' But this the driver didn't approve so he got off the footplate too and together they walked back repeating what Charlie had done. Eventually at the twelfth wagon they found what Charlie should have found before, that the vacuum hose pipe was not properly seated on the plug and was admitting air. Charlie went between the wagons, reseated the plug and emerged into the darkness of the tunnel.

As he did so, he heard from the front end: 'Ch . . . ch . . . ch . . . ch . . . ch . . . ch . . . ch . . . ch . . . ch . . . ch . . . ch. Not only had the driver left the big ejector on but he had left the regulator open – or so we found at the inquiry which I took the next day. The driver and Charlie set off like crazy to catch the engine but in a minute or so the wagons began to shoulder past them; anyway Charlie caught his handlamp between his knees, came a purler and the driver fell over him.

By the time they had picked themselves up the brake van had gone by and although they shouted the door was shut and there was no response. They clawed their way to the nearest signal and telephoned to the signalman at Waverley. He, good lad, had three choices: first to let the train go on its way to Portobello but the line was full of trains; secondly to direct it to the line to Granton Dock which was empty; third to turn it up a dead end and wreck it against a wall of rock. He rightly chose the second. Next, how to warn the guard. So he rang the station inspector who proceeded to instant action. He gathered a posse of carriage cleaners, mainly female, ticket collectors and porters and posted them half-way along the platform.

In a minute or so the train emerged from Haymarket tunnel, now going strong, maybe 25 miles an hour. The guard emerged from his brake and leaned over the rear rail, his cap on the side of his head and his pipe drawing sweetly. It was Angus Panton's day. He had an early turn. He would be at Portobello about noon. He had arranged to take his wife and kids out for the afternoon and evening. It was his birthday. Therefore when the mob on the platform screamed in every key and in every range from soprano to basso profundo: 'Ye're on the road to Granton. There's naeone on the fuitplate' he thought they were shouting: 'Hurrah for Angus Panton. Many Happy Returns, mate.' At least that is what he told the inquiry.

I believed every word of it. If I hadn't, neither he nor I could have done anything about it. It is, in passing, a dilemma common for all chairmen of inquiries, what to believe from your witnesses. Sometimes of course they do not attend. They are dead. Sometimes – often – they lie like troopers; you can be sure that if, no, when, a driver and his fireman tell the same tale it is not corroboration but collaboration. Sometimes members of the same trade hang together. Once after an accident at Welwyn Garden City it was obvious beyond peradventure that the driver of the up Aberdonian had ignored the outer home signal at danger and had run into the back of a local from Baldock in the platform. He and his fireman attested that the signal shewed a full green light. What is more, the driver – a well known, well-liked and well-met character in New England loco – organised over the next few weeks a succession of his mates who reported repeatedly that they had passed this signal at green only to find the inner home signal at red.

Swearing oaths, unusual even for him, W.E. (Buster) Green, the District Superintendent at Kings Cross, held at my behest an inquiry into each and every one. Unfortunately the original driver of the Aberdonian had not briefed his clique too well, so that Bill Green ended up with a hotch-potch of stories that the signal in question was at Welwyn North, at Hatfield and even not on the up road but the down. Nevertheless, I do not claim that in my reports on inquiries I always believed the right people.

The best boss I ever had was Colonel H. H. Maudlin; as a green District Superintendent I once consulted him about a case in which a goods guard was accused of 'propositioning' a woman on a late night train between Cambridge and St Ives. The old man laughed fatly and said: 'Tell Jerry that he leaves the court without a stain on his character. Tell him also not to do it again. And to make sure don't roster him on passenger trains.'

But back to Angus Panton and to his response to the cries of 'Ye're on the r-road to Granton . . .' He took the pipe out of his mouth, took off his cap and beamed largely on the capering mob on the platform. It was not until he found himself, not in the short tunnel heading to Portobello but in the rock cutting leading to Granton that it dawned on him that something was amiss.

Now in these days of trains with brakes continuous from engine to brake van, if any, all that a guard has to do in order to stop his train is to pull the tap. On go the brakes and the driver looks back wondering 'what the hell . . . ?' In 1939 Angus thought slowly and remembered Rule 127 which provided that if a guard wishes to draw the attention of the driver he must screw on his handbrake and release it sharply. In this case the driver and Charlie having just trudged out of Haymarket tunnel, Rule 127 had no effect.

Angus was now in a serious dilemma. He was on a severe down gradient. Speed was increasing rapidly, maybe fifty miles an hour. He thought slowly and deeply. If he stuck to what was to prove literally to be a sinking ship he might drown. If on the other hand the engine and a few wagons went into the dock but the rear of the train remained on terra firma he would be badly shaken up but no worse. If he got off the train at fifty plus miles an hour there was no knowing what the harvest would be. When next day I asked him, why he had chosen as he did, he pondered for a long time and said: 'We-e-ll when I was a lad I used to jump off tr-a-a-a-ins!' However that may be, he collected his traps, threw them on to the low cutting through which the train was hurtling. Then he lowered himself on to the bottom step and he alighted. He slightly twisted his left ankle.

1940

We celebrate – not enough indeed – what the railways contributed to D Day in 1944. We enjoy the memory of getting the crowds home after the jamboree of VE day. The year 1940 has gone largely unsung. Well, it is going to have a piece to itself here, first because in no other year of the war did so many things happen from the phoney war to blitzkreig, to Battle of Britain, to the blitz at night. Secondly because in no year of the war was there so great a surge of common feeling. I use the word 'patriotism' reluctantly because we are not that sort of people. But there is an emotion beyond the call of duty which led a driver of a train of bombs, one wagon of which was on fire, to go back, pick up the wagon and drive like hell out of the Cambridgeshire village through which he was passing. A minute or so later he was blown to smithereens.

Driver Gimbert, George Cross. Thirdly the Cambridge district where I spent most of the year was unusually the hinge of the war. We were the area in which the battles of destruction would be fought if it happened that the invasion Sea Lion ever was attempted, and we were the focus of our next offensive, the bomber campaign. We were building aerodromes like crazy. Millions of tons of bricks, cement, aggregates, reinforcing steel rods were focussing on us from all over the land. Finally, it was a year more than any other in which one absurdity in our life followed another.

We began 1940, Norrie and I, at 9 Delta Place, Inveresk. Hogmanay was a foul, raw, foggy evening thawing after several days' frost. We were sitting in our upstairs room in front of a large bright fire of Lothian coal at twenty-one shillings a ton. At about ten o'clock we heard a dull thud downstairs. Norrie said: 'It would be funny if that was the kitchen ceiling'. I laughed carelessly. But after a couple of minutes went down to look. It *was* the kitchen ceiling. Water was cascading down the gap and through a trapdoor close by. Like the supreme idiot I am I did not know where the main stop-cock was. Norrie joined me. I looked at her. 'There may be something to turn off up there – I'm too big to get through that trapdoor. You might . . .' She blanched but gallantly climbed on the kitchen table. I gave her a shoulder. Up she went. And in a minute or two all was peace. Then the problem was a plumber. Norrie, drying off in the bathroom said: 'On Hogmanay? Don't be ridiculous.' I said, I'll go from pub to pub . . .' And rugged up, I went out with the raw fog. At the corner of Inveresk Place and the main road I literally marched full tilt into a little man. He went flying into the gutter. He was cheerful and friendly in spite of my having done him grievous bodily harm. I brushed him down and said tentatively: 'We are in trouble at home. Can you possibly tell me where I can find a plumber?' This godsend answered: 'I *am* a plumber.' He fetched his tools and spent till three o'clock in the morning putting us to rights. Norrie who assumes command of industrial relations in our house kept passing him wee drams up through the trap door. He went home mouthing barbaric

Celtic songs but the joints which he had wiped stayed wiped.

At that time I was in Edinburgh as Assistant District Superintendent. I did not like their attitude to managing. Too many hammers cracking small nuts. Certainly they ran their trains to time. They had got that message through loud and clear to all their staff. And the outcome was one with which I was wholly in tune. I was less in tune with my compulsory part in a minor incident on a sleeping-car train. The MacTurk or The MacGuinness or some such had complained to the General Manager (instead of to the sleeping car attendant) about some item of equipment missing from his berth. Assistant Superintendent to District Superintendent: 'For the next three weeks the Assistant District Superintendent will inspect all sleeping cars at Waverley Station'. On three nights a week. Norrie said: 'Absurd – just don't do it.' My rosy-cheeked boss with his white moustache and halo (no less) of white hair said: 'Mphm' which made clear his disapproval but went on to advise me that if I didn't do what H. G. Sayers said, he, H. G. Sayers, would make my life a burden. So for three weeks I went down to Waverley. Now of all railwaymen sleeping car attendents are the ones who cherish their jobs. I have heard through the grape-vine of a member of Parliament who regularly wetted her bed. But no attendant made anything official of it. They have a good basic wage, regular overtime and a very large take indeed from tips. So I made a black list of the very few people who had made any complaint in the last year, went down to Waverley, looked at the passenger list on each door and if no MacTurk appeared I said to the attendant: 'Good evening Joe' and passed on. If the MacTurk was on the list I said: 'I see you've got the MacTurk to-night' and often enough got some reply such as: 'And I hope we get a rough stop at Newcastle just as he is using his potty'. So that passed off in peace.

So there was not enough to do; well, enough real things to do. Certainly I was overworked but apart from the peace-time chores it was seeing that the right number of tin hats got to the stations, inspecting the lighting in marshalling yards and so on.

Then, as so often, relief came suddenly. A V2 2–6–2 had dropped off the road, all engine wheels and tender wheels one night as it went into Haymarket loco. I watched the breakdown gang labouring manfully and with skill to put her back on the road, which they had done by about three o'clock in the morning. As usual, we repaired to the Accident Van for a self-congratulatory mug of tea and a huge step of corned beef sandwich when Rattle-Rattle-Thump and the V2 was off the road again. The gang turned to and had her on the road by 7.30. I made my way home, had a bath and breakfast, listened to the kids, Jeremy 2½ and Joslin. Jeremy was a piece of quicksilver, an all dancing, all singing, all talking act. I was never allowed to get by without hearing his long and accurate account of what the milkman and the postman had said to Norrie and him and what the other events of the day had been. Therefore it was around nine o'clock when I got to bed.

At about nine-thirty H. G. Sayers came on the phone. Usually his messages came through my boss. So that in itself shewed something. 'I want your husband to take an inquiry into that derailment of a V2 and I want the report with the evidence in triplicate this afternoon.'

Norrie said: 'He has only just gone to bed.'

'Never mind – wake him. There's a war on.' Not, I thought later, in the Edinburgh District, nor would reports in triplicate do much towards winning it. Norrie, who was a warrior, said: 'I'll tell him when he wakes up.'

'Tell him now.'

'I'll tell him when he wakes up.'

I woke at four o'clock in the afternoon. Norrie was hugging herself with glee.

The next morning, believe it or not, we had another derailment – this time 'round the Sub', the Edinburgh south side loop suburban passenger line. About noon came a message: 'Mr Gardiner wishes to see Mr Fiennes at once.' H. G. Sayers had served John the Baptist's head to Herod on a charger. On my way, scrubbed my shoes and cleaned my face and hands as best I could. With the best will in the world no one can avoid pulling things and lifting things and climbing about at derailments. So one's extremities and office suit do not look as they should before Herod.

R. D. Gardiner was a large, benign man. He smiled on me. 'Fiennes', he said, 'The District Superintendent at Cambridge has had a nervous breakdown. Colonel Maudlin (Superintendent of the former Great Eastern area) has asked for you to go and take charge of the District. How quickly can you get there?'

'To-morrow' I cried. And I took the V2 inquiry before I went.

George Sutcliffe, District Superintendent at Cambridge was not in fact off duty but was certainly not in charge. He swayed a little as he moved. He was hesitant in speech. His hands were large with rheumatism. His eyes were bulbous and opaque. Reuben Taylor and I used to look out some task each evening for George to do next day in the farthest confines of the District – Sutton Bridge or Hunstanton or Earls Colne. George used to set off in his Rover and be back sometime. The story has a happy ending. Fifteen months later George was back firmly in the saddle.

The former Assistant District Superintendent, A. H. (Bertie) Wright, had just retired. The District was being effectively run by Chief Controller (or District Inspector) George Docking. The Cambridge District was unique among all other in British railways for demanding ingenuity and quick action. The freight service was static for hardly a day. In March flowers; in June strawberries; in July raspberries; in August plums; all interspersed with peas and carrots and potatoes. The question was often not what do we do next month? but what do we do to-morrow? In June for instance, given a couple of days of sunshine, the number of wagons of strawberries loaded rose from sixty to six hundred. George Docking was a supreme master of these ingenuities.

The problem, was the flood of materials for building aerodromes for the bomber offensive. George had allocated March up yard. Bricks, cement, aggregate, reinforcing rods were stashed away each in its own siding. A demand from a site could be met within three or four hours. Alas, the part of the problem which was not the railway's was that a wet winter had bogged down cranes and tractors on the site so that unloading had been abysmally slow. George had not felt that he had enough clout to demand remedies at a high level. I thought 'Hell – why not try?' so we demanded a meeting with the contractors, the Ministry of Supply and the RAF. A surprising number of Brass turned up. We took them to Feltwell, for Brandon Railway Yard was clogged with traffic waiting to be unloaded. The field itself was littered with bogged down cranes, tractors and trailers. Nothing moved. We hardly needed to speak.

What was more surprising was that within a week every site had caterpillar cranes, great tractors with spiked wheels, spare timber cuts and trailers. The trickle of traffic out of March up yard became an avalanche. And by the autumn the Stirlings and Halifaxes and Lancasters had flown in and were giving the Hun a bit of his own back. It was a pity that it took the RAF so long to discover how to hit anything useful.

The next contribution to the war effort, if negative, was also about hitting something. The Colonel telephoned one afternoon and said: 'The RAF have bombed Hamm marshalling yards nineteen nights running and can't understand why they keep working'. I said: 'I will take them down to Whitemoor and let them talk to Ingham.'

The Colonel laughed fatly: 'That should be good.' So next day a very point-of-vice Air Commodore and a Squadron Leader arrived. After the preliminaries the Squadron Leader said: 'The quickest and surest way of paralysing a country's war effort is to disrupt its transport between the producing factories and the armed forces.'

'Sherry' I said.

The Air Commodore sat up as if shot. There had been a leak of catastrophic proportions.

'Relax' I said. 'Those words were obviously written by an economist – one who enunciates absolutely incontrovertible principles. The trouble with Sherry is that having been in Headquarters offices all his life he has not the remotest notion whether they can be made to work. Sherry. Come on –

let's go down to Whitemoor.'

And in companionable silence we did, lunched frugally at the Griffin and arrived in Yardmaster Ingham's office. Ingham was a vast countryman with plate-sized hands and size twelve black boots. He was nobody's fool. When the Air Commodore had told him the story we went across to the tower which controls the points and the retarders in the up yard. Ingham said: 'Well, what sort of picture would the yardmaster at Hamm have after a visit from your aircraft?'.

The Squadron Leader took a hand in this. 'There would be thirty or forty wagons damaged and derailed. There would be maybe thirty craters in the sidings, say twenty feet across and ten feet deep.'

'Fair enough' said Ingham. 'So before midnight when the All Clear goes the Yardmaster gets out the cranes from the Locos, say four of them. By 2am the wagons are clear. Then follows a train of locomotive ashes and large gangs of men. They fill in the holes, run a bulldozer over the top, lay track; say six hours work.'

'So when our reconnaisance aircraft goes over at 11am . . .'

'Precisely.'

We walked back to Ingham's office in silence. Then the Air Commodore said: 'Well, what do we do?'

'Give it up' said Ingham flatly.

'The Air Council won't like that – they are set on wining the war this way.'

'Look' said Ingham, 'We have had the experience of generations in getting round blockages by accidents. There are usually several ways round. Why should a few bombs be any different?'

I came in then. I said: 'The most vulnerable bits of a railway are bridges and viaducts. But even then the interruption is short. The other day a Hun aircraft came at Audley End viaduct, right down on the deck, one bomb actually landed on the viaduct, skidded across it and down the bank on the other side. Duddell, the stationmaster, was seen rushing after the Hun calling down curses on his head. But suppose that bomb had exploded; within half an hour the freight traffic would have been diverted via Chelsford on the east side and via Hitchin on the west. It might take two days to get a temporary trestle across and resume normal working.'

It was Ingham who landed the final punch. He said: 'The Huns aren't going for our railways. Maybe on the general staff there is a gruppenfuhrer who was once a yardmaster.' We heard no more of Hamm. I wonder if the yardmaster there ever found out that he had Ingham to thank.

One Sunday we sat in brother John's garden near Bishops Stortford. Faraway drums were beating, the drums of Dunkirk. In a few days the men began to come through in dribs and drabs; unshaven, unwashed, unarmed, exhausted, numb. Some of them stayed with us for a day or two before going on to units. Jeremy welcomed this procession. He climbed on them, pulled at the tufts and in fact did a good deal toward bringing them back to consciousness. The restoration of the army to consciousness was not for the railways an unmixed blessing. They now had to prevent the German invasion in East Anglia. So pill-boxes sprang up anywhere – not so bad but messages came through that they were starting to erect tank traps on all the bridges where the railway crossed a river. Luckily someone had appointed to me a Railway Liaison Officer, a Major Selby. We agreed that in an emergency we would derail an engine on each bridge and the Hun tanks could make of those what they chose. So he spoke words and the nuisance abated. We also had an armoured train – there is glory for you, officered and manned by Poles. They worked between Kings Lynn and Hunstanton, where they faced only Lincolnshire across the Wash. But they did nobody any harm except me when the officers in a body came to Cambridge 'to report' and drank double whiskies to an extent which no railway officer could afford. Eventually I told the Colonel and received a dispensation.

During the month's interlude we formed, naturally, a company of the Local Defence Volunteers, later Home Guard, later 'Dad's Army'. Our OC was Major Henry Love, head of our works section. We received seventy-seven pikes and three rifles. I applied for a rifle, but as Private Fiennes this plea cut no ice. It would have had to be a very unwary Hun who let me get at him with my pike. However, we drilled and brandished in the style of Agincourt. And we had a practice shoot. I renewed my application for a rifle and got one. This led to an incident, not very creditable. My office overlooked the platform at Cambridge. One afternoon a string of bombs exploded at the north end of the station. There came the roar of an aircraft flying up the main line. I jumped for the rifle, got a round up the spout, opened the window. The wing of the aircraft was maybe fifteen feet from me; the pilot maybe thirty feet. I cuddled the rifle, got my eye into the 'V', drew a bead on the pilot and lovingly squeezed the trigger. He flew straight on, lifted over Hills Road bridge and so back to Germany. Nevertheless, I had fired a shot in anger which is more than many of my friends did in six years in the 'army'.

The Cambridge District was now well on top of its job, and the next major event, the Battle of Britain, had little effect on us with no more than weaving contrails in the sky, occasionally a wrecked aircraft. We had two RAF fighter stations, at Debden and Duxford. The Huns had a go at both. I was involved in one. I was cycling to work on Shelford Hill when suddenly there was a stunning clamour of engines and gunfire. A wave of Stukas streaking eastwards lifted just over the road. The Hurricanes slightly higher and much faster were making short pounces on them. In no time at all there was silence, the only relic of the speed and violence was three columns of flame and smoke in the fields. I heard later that one Hurricane had shot down seven out of the twelve.

Then, the battle won, we settled down to the long haul of the night blitz. In this our neighbour the Stratford District was directly involved. Again the Huns made no direct and concerted attack on railways but the general fall of bombs slowed movement. Each morning Stratford had many trains, which control had stopped overnight, to pick up and get into the marshalling yards. I said to George Docking: 'What can we do to help?' George said, after reflection: 'We can keep some traffic out of London altogether. If the Norwich District and ourselves trapped all the Great Western traffic at

Cambridge and ran it via Bletchley and Oxford it would help a bit.' So, foolishly, I took myself off to Stratford with this proposal to see the District Superintendent F. (for Freddie) C. 'Musso' (appearance and attitude) Wilson. Freddie thanked me kindly and we put in the proposal next day. One never did anything the *same* day if the Great Western was one of the parties. Then I made my mistake. I said to Freddie: 'May I go home on a goods train from Temple Mills?' Freddie said laconically: 'Bombers' Moon'. 'If you can do it every night I ought to be able put up with one.'

So we had a snack in the refreshment room at Stratford and I walked down to the yardmaster's office. The Yardmaster was Dan Rose. He had earned a Military Medal in the Kaiser's war, which you didn't get for anything trivial. He was tough, wiry, dark, hot-eyed. He wasn't a leader – he was a driver and his staff went in fear of him. He was the right man in the right place. I said: 'What do you do when you get an Air Raid Red?' 'We keep going' he said. 'If there is a lot of stuff coming down really close we knock off for a few minutes. What troubles us is that we can't use lights so it's all pretty slow.' At that moment we were walking across to the Cambridge yard. The sirens wailed. The lights went out; and the guns began to rave. It got a bit lighter. The searchlights – it seemed hundreds of them, were pencilling and roaming and criss-crossing in the sky. Once one pin-pointed an aircraft. Instantly four or five others fixed on the spot. Clusters of spangles of anti-aircraft fire surrounded the spot. But the aircraft dived and climbed and wheeled apparently unharmed. We began to hear the distant whistle of bombs and faraway crumps.

Dan led me up to an engine, our old Great Eastern six-coupled workhorse, a J17. No one of course in view. Tarpaulins fell on both sides of the cab; another stretched from the roof of the cab to the tender so that the light from the firehole door was cut off. Dan beat on the side. A corner was lifted and a face appeared. 'Bill Andrews' said Dan. 'This is Mr Fiennes, District Superintendent Cambridge. He wants to ride back home to Shelford. 'Wiv us?' said Bill and decided not to add: 'he must be crazy'. He handed me a large roll of cotton waste. I clambered aboard into this hole containing now three men in a space say five feet by four and a fire big enough and hot enough to heat the Albert Hall.

In the original single line bores of Woodhead tunnel on the footplate of engines starting on a greasy day from the loop I have been down on my knees with a wet handkerchief over my nose and mouth praying interminably for the dawn of Dunford Bridge, but never in my wildest dreams had I imagined that there could be any heat and airlessness as there was on that footplate. And that is what the Stratford enginemen were going through for, say, four hours a night. Bill heard a shout: set back'. He could of course not see where he was going so the shunter called 'Thirty yards . . . twenty . . . ten . . . five.' The shunter coupled up, shouted: 'You've got the guard's signal . . . 'Right away.' and Bill opened the regulator gently, collected his train and took it steadily down the goods line toward the junction with the Cambridge Main Line at Copper Mill.

Tottenham stopped us at his home signal. I said to Bill: 'Shall I carry out Rule 55 for you?' Bill, who did not seem to have had Rule 55 on his mind nodded. So I went into the signalbox and wrote in the train register book: '8.55pm Rule 55. 8.00pm. Temple Mills to Whitemoor. G. F. Fiennes.' After some time, without actually saying anything I got the signalman to put a lever collar on his home signal. By now the whistles and crumps were all around us. A timber yard near the furniture factory was burning and the Huns were obviously viewing it as a mark. All very daunting but the signalman seemed to be taking it in his stride. Suddenly came an enormous, stunning explosion. 'Parachute mine' said the signalman. 'Somewhere over by Enfield.' 'How do we get out of here?' I said. He went on to Control. Then he said: 'Well, the main line is full of trains and one of them is in trouble in Enfield Lock. So no use that way; the Goods Lines are clearing. I'll put you down to Pickets Lock. We trundled safely past the burning timber yard and slowly but uneventfully on to Broxbourne where the All Clear had gone and we could breath again. I never went near the London blitz again until I became District Superintendent, Stratford, myself and 'enjoyed' the V1 doodlebugs and the V2 rockets.

In the background of every activity at this time – August and September – was the prospect of a German invasion. True, we had won the Battle of Britain and it seemed crazy that the Hun should attempt a crossing in the teeth of the Navy and without command of the air. Nevertheless the planners had produced a most splendid plan whereby on an Alert the principal towns of the East Coast were to be evacuated to attractive places like Wellingborough and Kettering. So on the word 'Go' all the suburban trains in London after the evening peak would make tracks for Cromer, Yarmouth, Lowestoft, Aldeburgh, Felixstowe, Harwich, Walton-on-the-Naze, Clacton and so on – about 200 trains.

They were, of course, non-lavatory stock. And Norrie began to doubt my sanity when she found me outside the loo, which she had entered, with a stop-watch in my hand. I was in fact trying to answer the question: 'how many temporary loos do we need to erect at Newmarket, Ely and so on in order to make a train load of 1000 people comfortable in ten minutes?' We erected the loos, hessian over timber frames. No doors. No segregation of the sexes. There was a war on. So the plan was made and all was ready.

At this moment it came into my head that I would like a couple of days off. So we parked Jeremy and Joslin with brother John near Bishops Stortford, hired a sailing craft from H. C. Banham and set off down the Ouse, promising to let George Docking know where we stopped. We had a slashing sail down to Ely, moored near Ely Dock Junction, told the signalman where we would be and moored a couple of hundred yards upstream to a snug spot. About 11pm came a hammering on the roof of the cabin. The telegraph lad from Ely Dock Junction. 'The alert has gone out for the East Coast evacuation, starting at 6am to-morrow. Mr Docking says that everything is under control – not to hurry back.'

Norrie and I conferred. It was a glorious, still night. The

river was a sheet of silver. On the river it would take us less than three hours to Cambridge. We set off. Now this was a time when the Home Guard was very trigger-happy. Parachutists were reported nightly; but how they could in their wildest dreams have expected the German Navy thirty miles up the Ouse has always defeated me. Nevertheless we swept round a bend at some six knots and there closely in front of us was a hawser stretched from bank to bank with a large keg in the centre surmounted by a red flag. We charged it as far as possible from the flag. Some securing device in the bank ripped out and the whole enterprise sank without trace. I said to Norrie: 'Nelson could not have done better.'

We got to Banhams. She dropped me at control and went on home. Then we waited on events. It turned out to be a splendid and typically East Anglian non-event. In the coastal towns the church bells were to bawl an alarm. The mayors and corporations in chains and robes, preceded by their mace-bearers were to march (several times) to the station accompanied by the town bands blowing martial music. All was done to remove the citizenry from danger and to give them a splendid send-off. Presently the reports began to come in: 6.15am Lowestoft 23, 6.20 Felixstowe 19 . . . I said: Does this mean the number of people aboard?' 'I suppose so' said George Docking. Then came 6.30am Aldeburgh cancelled.' By 8am the whole enterprise had been abandoned. Having now lived in East Anglia for twenty years I know they just didn't believe in a German invasion. And they weren't going to budge – if Whitehall did believe in one. How right they were.

The other two events of 1940 were both personal. As Christmas approached we received from Sir Michael Barrington-Ward, Chairman of the Railway Executive, one of those ukases for which he was renowned. 'In the national interest no special trains shall be run during the Christmas period.' I conferred with George Unwin. George was a very large District Inspector. His face was as near a peony in flower than a face. I remember once in a pub at Wisbech a little man kept darting glances at him. Eventually he spoke: 'I do 'ope we shan't get any of they late frosts, or you'll be cut down.'

'George' I said, 'if we are not to run any specials how are we to get all those thousands of Irishmen working on the aerodromes home?'

George said: 'I've been thinking about that. You know, Cambridge carriage sidings are pretty congested. I'll get a couple of sets stabled at Ely where there is plenty of room.'

I had done right to talk to George Unwin rather than Chief Controller George Docking. Docking, although a masterpiece of ingenuity, went often enough by the book. George Unwin's reputation was 'Don't do as I do. Do as I say.' He was a master of short cuts.

Anyway, on the evening of Christmas Eve George Unwin and I betook ourselves to Ely, a focal point for what was about to happen. A terminating train from Norwich ran in. The Irish spilled out, hared for the refreshment room and drank it dry. Then with money in their pockets and caring for neither God nor man they stood four deep along the platform. The express from Hunstanton to London ran in packed to the hatches. There was a kind of silent heave and seven hundred and fifty English were on the platform. A thousand Irish were in the train. Nobody attempted to dispute the situation so the guard gave the right away and away she went.

Then I became official. 'George' I said, 'We have a contractual obligation to get passengers home and dry by the last train in the evening. Was that the last train in the evening?'

'Yes Sir' said George.

'Well is there anything we can do to carry out our duty?'

'Well, Sir, there are a couple of spare sets in Ely yard.'

'Then that is what we must do.' And we did. And we reported ourselves to the Colonel who laughed fatly. I think he enjoyed telling Barrington-Ward whom he did not like overmuch.

The other item was one of no considerable importance to the war effort. It seems funny to think of now but in 1940 we were still taking poison gas seriously. As District Air Raid Precautions Officer I used to go round the District, practising gangs in decontaminating locomotives or yards from mustard gas, phosgene and the like. On this Sunday I set off for Kings Lynn. Norrie's brother Sam came with me. We had a little old Ford 10. There was a sharp frost. Somewhere short of Ely a precisely similar black Ford 10 got into a skid two hundred yards away, careered across the road and back and the second time hit us opposite the driver's door. He finished up upside down in a ditch. 'That chap's a gonner' said the Reverend Samuel Davies without emotion. We crossed the road. Petrol was pouring from the tank which was just in front of the windshield. We righted the car, tore open the door and out clambered a man smoking a cigarette. 'Thanks' he said. 'Pity. I am a policeman and this is my Sergeant's car.' Then he set off to make what peace he could.

So, 1940 came to an end. The best year of my railway service except maybe the years at Paddington. The sense of being at full stretch. The freedom which anyone who served old Colonel Maudlin enjoyed. The knowledge that the Cambridge District was doing something extremely useful and doing it well. The sense of a trained staff all pulling in the same direction. The absurdities which in spite of 'Don't you know there's a war on' kept on enlivening the proceedings. In 1940, once we had left Scotland, we were happy indeed.

4

Great Eastern –
The Post War Revival

NORWOOD YARD WHITEMOOR

23 April is my wife's and Shakespeare's, birthday. For six weeks until I too am forty-eight, she is as demonstrably for promotion senior to, as she is always more suitable than, me. And in these six weeks, by custom, openly, and with no lip-service to her vow to obey, she may do just as she pleases.

What she pleased twenty years ago, the year we married, was to drive an engine. On high days and holidays, when there was only a skeleton staff about, we went down in the evening to Norwood Yard at Whitemoor and, very high and mighty in the cab, she shunted the Fast Goods. I sat in the office nearby with my hands over my ears, not to hear the rattle of point rodding and the crunch of wheels on timber as she got off the road. If she did, no one ever told me. I never looked for marks. And so we never incurred the just wrath of our Lords and Masters at Cambridge.

Norwood, too, has just passed an anniversary: a melancholy one: the first after its demotion from an Express Goods Yard to shunting empties. A sorry end for what has been, I myself believe, the fastest yard in Britain and may be in the world. I have heard that between six o'clock and half past eight they have put more than seven hundred wagons of fruit over the little hump.

Over six hundred in two and a half hours I have seen myself, in the heat and glow of an autumn evening. The Wisbeches and Lynns, the Norwiches and Londons, the Sutton, the Loops, the Parkeston, surging thick and fast on to the Dirt Track. Happy Laws, the regular guard on the Parkeston, *point-de-vice* in waxed moustache, carnation and gleaming boots – 'Would you speak seriously to Mr Gibb (the Assistant Yardmaster) about his language?' Yes, I would – and did. How undignified for the godfather of our eldest boy.

The staff on the Dirt Track, releasing train engines, breaking vacuum pipes, pulling the cords, slackening screw couplings. Tommy, the burly head shunter, idle between trains, hands crossed on the top of his pole, chin resting on his hands; no collar, sweating like a bull, grimed up to his eyebrows. Nine minutes shunting, two minutes for the pilot to fetch another one; two hundred and fifty wagons an hour.

The long line of hooded vans rolls steadily over the little hump. The cuts peel off. Hodge in the ground-frame smacks the levers over and home. No countryman, Hodge, but a Cockney. And the coolest hand in the outfit in spite of his twenty lever movements a minute; in spite of the knowledge that in one half-second's error of judgement one cut will overtake another on a diverging route and twiddle both off the road; in spite of having to keep one eye to his right on the cuts and the other to his left on Tommy giving him the 'Tips' which siding the next cut is for.

Tommy and Hodge had their own private system of 'Tips', different from the other shifts. It is not easy to devise fifteen signals for the right hand – the left being occupied with the pole – which are not already in the Rule Book. Tapping the head, the shoulder, and scratching the armpit are three gestures which brought no blush of shame to the innocent cheek of visiting Top Brass, but for others Tommy and Hodge had drawn freely on their imagination.

The Colonel, then Superintendent (now dead and gone, more's the pity) greeted Tommy's system with abandoned chuckles, but times changed. A new yardmaster laid the dead hand of standardisation on Tommy and Hodge. And the more vivid expressions of their personalities were no more.

At half past seven two K3s slide into the engine line for the 7.45 Guide Bridge and 7.50 Ducie Street. The Control phone in the ground-frame rings.

'Nah, Mister' barks a voice. I hold the receiver an inch

further from my ear. 'Na-a-ah, mister, wheer's t'7.45?'

'We'll be a few minutes yet, Bill; we've still the Norwich to shunt and the fitted to pick up.'

'Will ye be la-a-te?'

'About five minutes, Bill.'

'Put shunter on t'phone'.

'If I do that Bill,' mildly, 'we shall be later still'.

Yorkshire changes the bowling. 'Ah'll have to send Percy Baynes back to show ye how to shunt'.

Percy Baynes, then a Guard; tall as a lamp-post, lean as a rail. A shunting pole looked like a tooth pick in his hand. He always uncoupled one handed, the pole resting delicately in his fingers, his forearm along the shaft. Three links, instanters, screw couplings, however stiff, yielded at once to the lithe bow of his body and the pressure on his elbow. He was never in a hurry in a yard. He seldom merely timed his trains. He had time in hand.

The last wagon of the Norwich rolls into No 11 for Ducic Street. The wheels ring high and sweet on the curve. Dick Green, the chaser, hatchet faced, lanky, stands at ease, indifferent, twirling his brake stick. Suddenly he turns. In two panther-like bounds he is up with it. The brake handle goes down.

Tommy sends the Pilot down for the fitted sections. Ten minutes rest while the Guide Bridge and the Manchester are made up and leave. The staff waddle to the ground-frame and sink on to the bench outside. This waddle is the outward and visible sign of the Fathers of March. Kangaroos carry their young in their breast pockets; Malays on their hips; the Fathers of March on triangular seats on the crossbars of their bicycles. Whereby their knees must revolve outside the handlebars, a habit comely in itself and lending in time an elegance to their walk.

The Guide Bridge and the Manchester have gone. There are still the 3.38 Lynn, the second Cambridge and the Whittlesea to shunt. At 8.25 Tommy has done. He sends his Pilot down 7 to pick up the Leicesters, Godleys and Lincolns for second sorting on to the front of the Colwick, the third Manchester and the Sheffield. His walk as he rolls back to the frame is of more-than-paternal elegance. He crosses his hands on the top of his pole and rests his chin on his hands. For more than an hour the Newcastle, the York, the Bradford and the rest, stream away lumping heavily over the little hump and heading towards the North. That was twenty years ago. Tommy, my wife, and Norwood will shunt no more Fast Goods in the heat and glow of an autumn evening.

HIGH POLITICS

'And the privilege and pleasure
   Which we treasure beyond measure
   Is to run on little errands for our Ministers of State.'
So wrote W. S. Gilbert in *The Gondoliers*, but read on.

Ena had got me pretty well organised. When she came in with the day's bundle of fun, the Control records of the running of the express passenger trains lay on top; then those of the express freights; then the local passenger trains, branch by branch; then the Control log; finally the letters. She never quite got round to sorting the letters into those which I should answer myself and those which I should not; nor indeed to producing the first category with the answers already typed, but this was only a matter of time. I would have done better if it had been so because occasionally I talked out of turn to someone who took it the wrong way and she would never have allowed that to happen.

On this particular morning, unusually, the pile was crowned by a thick cream laid envelope. Beneath it was a thick cream laid letter. Ena said: 'This came by hand a few minutes ago. The messenger wanted to wait for an answer but I got rid of him.' This was another of Ena's supreme talents, to get rid of people without them knowing that they were being got rid of. I reached for the letter and turned to the second page. It was signed 'squiggle', 'Minister of State, Ministry of Transport'. The one squiggle indicated that he was a Peer. And what with there having been fourteen Ministers of Transport in the last twelve years I felt no shame in not knowing the names of the Ministers of State. I turned back to the top page.

'Dear Mr Fiennes' it began. Well, he had bothered to find out my name.

'Last night I witnessed so dangerous an event on your District that I am convinced that your staff will not have appraised you of it. I feel it my duty to do so.'

I cocked my eye at Ena. 'So far' she said, 'so good. Its in the log.'

I read on: 'I was travelling after a dinner from Norwich to London when I was stopped by the level crossing gates being closed to the road at Rendham Crossing.'

'Ena' I said, 'the way from Norwich to London is up the A11 via Newmarket. What is Lord Squiggle doing sixty miles off his route at Rendham?' This was something to which Ena had no answer.

'Shortly' it read on 'a goods train came by at about forty miles an hour. Incredibily it had no engine. I blew my horn loudly but the crossing keeper did not appear and in five minutes the train reappeared travelling in the opposite direction, still with no engine. Then I got out of the car and demanded of the crossing keeper that he should open the gates, telling him who I was. He returned a surly answer. Once again the train went across the crossing, more slowly and on its return it came to rest blocking the road. Half an hour later it was removed by an engine. I demand', went on the noble lord, 'that an immediate enquiry be held into this extraordinary event and that you shall restore the standards of safety in your District which apply, I am glad to say, on other sections of British Railways.'

'Here' said Ena 'is the log.' It read: '11.15 Ipswich to Lowestoft while shunting at Witnesham ran back out of control and eventually came to rest across Rendham Crossing.'

'OK' I said, 'then the next thing is Danny' (the head of our accident section).

Danny appeared and because he was jealous of our safety record read the Minister of State's letter with growing disgust. By now I, having grasped what had happened, was chortling gently at the Minister having demonstrated before his eyes the principles of Sir Isaac Newton and becoming more perplexed with each demonstration. For Rendham Crossing being at the bottom of a valley, the railway climbing away steeply on each side, the train had trundled backwards and forwards until it had run out of steam – well, there had been no steam – had then run out of Sir Isaac Newton and come to rest across the path of the noble lord.

Danny recalled me. 'Had we better have an inquiry?'
'Yes' I said, 'to-morrow if it is suitable to Mr Carr (the Locomotive Superintendent) and Mr Ross (the engineer)'. Danny said: 'witnesses Driver, Fireman, Guard, Porter, Signalman and Crossing Keeper . . .'

So Danny arranged the inquiry. Ena wrote a letter regretting the Minister's experiences and telling him that we would let him know the results of the inquiry. She sent it by hand.

⋆　　⋆　　⋆

The inquiry was in due form. I as District Superintendent in the Chair, the Loco on my right, the engineer on my left. Danny on the engineer's left to keep order. A girl at each end of the table, taking verbatim notes. And opposite, the witness.

'You are William Moss, Goods Guard at Ipswich?'
'Yes.'
'And on the night of the 15th you were working the 11.15 Ipswich to Lowestoft with Driver Dean and Fireman Gotobed?'
'Yes.'
'Tell us what happened at Witnesham.'
'Well we had a heavy train. So we left the Brake and thirty-seven wagons in the platform. We went ahead with the Road Van, four wagons of cement and a hayrake for farmer Goodchild. We placed the cement and the hayrake in the cartage road. After that we took the road van into the shed. There is always a lot for Witnesham; cases of wine and

90

goodies from Fortnum & Mason and Harrods for the Hall; stock for the village shop; cartons for the Vicar. That took the best part of half an hour. Then we picked up three cement empties from the other cartage road, knocked them back on the train. And the whole train ran back toward Rendham Crossing.'

'How had you secured your brake van?'

'I can't have done, Guv'nor.' One thing about Bill Moss was that he worked things out and knew that there was no escaping that answer eventually. So he had come clean now.

'Why didn't you go back altogether, hook up the train and go?'

'Because we hadn't shunted the Coal Road.'

Fair enough. Well, there it was, the driver and fireman confirmed Bill's evidence. There was no fault in them. The signalman by telling and phoning the crossing keeper at Rendham had done his stuff. I asked him why he hadn't got aboard the brake van as it started to run back and stopped the whole brou-ha-ha but he said fairly enough that by the time he had got hold of the crossing keeper it was too late. Indeed, getting hold of the crossing keeper was the one thing which obviated all the elements of danger.

There remained the crossing keeper.

'You are Albert Strowger, crossing keeper at Rendham Crossing?'

'Yes.'

'Tell us what happened to the 11.15 from Ipswich on the night of the 15th.'

'Well the signalman at Witnesham told me that the rear of the train was running back. So I shut my gates and waited until she had run a couple of times through the crossing and then come to a stand. Then I phoned Witnesham and they came and fetched her.'

Then the inquiry took an unusual turn, but the Minister had himself made a point of his personal inconvenience.

'You had a customer.'

'Oh – 'im.'

'So you know him?'

'Yes, Lord—. He's often through. Maybe once a fortnight. He never uses the bridge a couple of miles away. He has to come blowing to get me out of bed at two o'clock.'

'Do you know where he goes?'

'Yes – up to the Hall.'

'Lady—?'

'No, the gardener. All of us round these parts know about it.'

With that we concluded the inquiry. We sent for Bill Moss. I reprimanded him severely which he took like a gentleman.

There remained a final little errand for the Minister of State.

'Dear Minister,

We have inquired into the circumstances of the event which inconvenienced you on the night of the 15th. One piece of gross carelessness set the events in train. The culprit has been identified and suitably punished. Apart from his error the rest of the staff acted correctly. There was at no time any danger to life or property.

Finally may I apologise that this last occasion of your use of Rendham Crossing should have inconvenienced you so greatly.'

The railway grapevine is a wonderful thing. News travels the length and breadth of the line without, so it seems, the written or spoken word. It pales into insignificance beside the secretaries' grapevine. Ena came in a couple of days later saying Albert Strowger will have no more disturbed nights. I tried to get more out of her but she closed up like an oyster and I never found out any more. 'Well' I said, 'I wonder whether he realises that one outcome of his demanding a full inquiry is that fifty or more copies of that inquiry verbatim are circulating round the District and Headquarters Offices of the LNER?'

Probably he didn't realise because reports and irregularities with freight trains, unlike those with passenger trains, were not sent to the Ministry. Nevertheless within a month we learned that never again would we have to run on little errands for that Minister of State.

THE LOUD COMPLAINT

Railways used to have a jargon for correspondence. No letter ended except with the words 'and have the goodness to do so-and-so and oblige yours faithfully . . .' Complaints were always loud and the recipient was always 'happy' to say that there was nothing in them. There was a yardmaster at Whitemoor, George Smith, who used to dance round the office flapping his wings crying: 'I am happy. . . . I am happy . . .' I was very quietly never happy in a letter again.

So in 1948 a Loud Complaint from our Commercial Manager: 'I have a loud complaint from a passenger and I may add he is a solicitor – that a nearly empty train passes through Ilford at 5.28. If this were stopped for him he would catch with ease his connection to Hastings whereas the normal train, the 5.31, presents a difficulty. Will you please let me know whether you can do this.'

Now at this stage you all need a lecture on timetabling but the short answer is that if once you depart from an interval timetable you will have done it twice, three times, four times in a year and your performance and punctuality which you cherish are in rags. So the Commercial Superintendent – and remember I was young, green and lacking in understanding – got a lecture on the art of timetabling. He replied – entirely within his rights: 'I did not ask you whether you would stop this train but whether you *could*.' And there I was backed into a corner. But I grabbed at a straw. I sent for W. R. Proctor, the Chief Ticket Inspector. In a couple of days time he came back grinning all over his face. 'Well I suppose you *could* call him a solicitor. He runs a sex shop in Ilford – appliances and all that; telephone numbers too. He comes down from Hastings about once a week.' A couple of telephone calls and the Loud Complaint evaporated into loud laughter.

Work in progress on electrification of GE section suburban services to Shenfield in 1949. Chadwell Heath Goods Yard signalbox is seen being demolished while the overhead catenary is almost complete.

OPENING THINGS

In a hundred years there has been very little change in the ceremony which attends a major railway advance. About five hundred guests, a special train, a banquet and inevitably the speeches. So it was when the first railway event took place, the opening of the electrification from Liverpool Street to Shenfield. Minister of Transport, Alfred Barnes, would cut a tape, be conducted to the cab, instructed what to do and drive the train merrily to Shenfield and back. My boss was the host and would be in the train. I as Assistant Superintendent would conduct the Minister. Easy for all. The Minister may have been reflecting that his father was a railway carter at Spitalfields market and what a nice change it was to be performing with passengers who loaded themselves on the hoof.

Anyway I successfully found the scissors; the tape fell apart at the first snip. We proceeded to the cab, got in, installed the Minister in the driver's seat and introduced him to the driver. Then I made my mistake. I took my eye off the ball.

The driver said: 'This on your left is the brake handle. This is the running position. This is the brake on.' And the Minister did it a couple of times.

94

'Now this on your right is the power controller. Round to the left for power off. Round to the right for power on.'

The Minister said: 'Like this?' and went into notch 3. We shot out of the station. I had just time to see that the signal was at clear. 'Keep going' I said to the driver, relaxed after a minute or so and in high good humour we proceeded to Shenfield and back. I approached Liverpool Street with some fear about what my boss might say but he was one of those who had been left on the platform. He had had an extra hour's drinking time.

So he declared the Shenfield Electrification well and truly opened. In six months a costing report showed it to be as

Inauguration of the Liverpool Street–Shenfield electrification. Minister of Transport Alfred Barnes cuts the tape. He later drove the first train which started a little too promptly and left some of the official party behind. (*British Railways*)

profitable as the Leeds and Newcastle Expresses, so down with those who say that commuter services can't pay. Sir Herbert Walker created a profitable Southern Railway on that basis. What you need is good equipment, a tight timetable and diagrams and first-class punctuality.

THE BRITANNIAS

'And now' said Stuart Ward, 'for the big one.'

I looked at him with utter incomprehension.

'Well, the Shenfield is in. We are top of the punctuality league by a mile. The diagrams are going to plan. The passenger-miles per train must be a record for anywhere. Now for the Main Line.'

He produced an envelope. 'This will be like falling off a log. Two round trips to Norwich a day – 460 miles.'

I interrupted: 'Is there any locomotive on BR that will do that? The B1s won't. They'll need coal every round trip and all those things which drivers do with flares and bundles of waste?'

'And you Chairman of the Locomotive Building Committee? Look, this came this morning. . . . 'New British Standard Express Locomotive, Route availability seven, tractive effort over 30,000 lb.'

'Gimme' I said. Yes, it was all there. 'For every 7MT doing two round trips we shall save two B1s plus spares so if we order 25 Class 7 MTs we need not order, say, fifty-five B1s.'

So a consultation with E. S. Cox at the British Railways Board, head of the Locomotive and Engines Committee. Yes, they would run all day and all night; four hundred and sixty miles a day was just the sort of job for them. I went to the Building Programme Committee. No one else made a bid and they were ours. Stuart bashed along with the diagrams – you see like the Shenfield this timetable wasn't a timetable – it was a series of engine diagrams. Only one gave us doubt. The last of the day brought up the 9.40 goods from Norwich to Spitalfields and went back with the 2.55 newspapers – the fastest and by far the train most susceptible to complaint. The

There is little doubt that the Deltic 3,300hp diesel electric locomotives with their sustained 100mph running, pushed the East Coast route expresses to the forefront in the 1960s, while the rival West Coast route lagged behind during electrification work.

9.40 Norwich was a notoriously bad runner. Eventually Stuart said: 'May not the upshot be that the Norwich becomes a good runner?' And so it was.

All went smoothly. Certainly the Commercial Superintendent bellyached that the Norfolkman which had left Liverpool Street at 10am for years would now be at 9.30. Certainly Frank Chilvers, Assistant at Stratford, said: 'Gerry, don't do it. The last time anyone changed the main line timetable was 1914 (40 years before) and you remember what happened to him. He got the sack. Then the blow fell. Barrington-Ward, the operating member of the Railway Executive, found out. 'What' he cried, 'send our first batch of express locomotives to that tramway? Never!' and wrote us telling us to do it with B1s. Alex Dunbar and I cogitated for hours. Eventually we made it short and sharp. 'The new timetable is due to start in three weeks. It is already in print.

No Britannias – no timetables.' He gave way, taking one to work the Continentals out of Victoria and one to Old Oak Common where they did not like it at all.

The ironic thing is that after three weeks the whole fleet was grounded because some defect in the axles allowed the wheels to turn faster than the axles which wasn't good for the motion. And for about a month we had to do just what we would have done if B1s had taken their place – namely use a lay-over B1 after each round trip.

Then they were back and ran a magnificent service. We even had a malignant triumph (for it still meant something in those days). Our Christmas card from Liverpool Street was a picture of the Broadsman at speed and subscribed: 'The fastest train in Britain.' Mind you within weeks the North Eastern took five minutes out of something between Darlington and York but we had had our little hour of glory.

The Deltics went of course even further, over 700 miles a day, but it was the Britannias which taught us that an engine diagram can be disguised as an express timetable and only a few people ever realised it.

EAST ANGLIAN FLOODS – JANUARY 1953

When we think of flooding what picture do we see? For me it is a rather crummy street with large puddles and the fire brigade pumping out the cellars and leaving tidy wives a filthy job of cleaning floors and carpets. Annually the rivers Exe, Severn, Ouse and Nene do this to hundreds of households up and down the land. Let me aver with no fear of contradiction that the East Anglian floods of 1953 were the greatest single railway disaster in history. As morning came we had no railway in East Anglia – well, you could get from Colchester to Sudbury and a few disconnected bits like that but no more. For the rest of the low-lying land, hundreds of square miles of it, was a sheet of wind-torn salt water.

It all began quietly enough. Control rang me to say that the Meteorological Office had put all coastguards on alert. 'There will be an exceptionally high tide to-night.' OK this happened every two or three years and a little water got into the yards at Wells. So I took no notice. Then it came: 'The sea has overtopped the sea wall at Skegness. It has inundated Butlins camp and several are drowned. When I eventually got on to Control I got a message: 'The combination of a high spring tide and a very low depression has caused a surge which may well overrun many coastal defences.' Then our Districts began to move locomotives and rolling stock to higher ground and to warn staff to get on to high ground at signs of trouble.

The first signs came soon. The Nene, the Ouse and the dykes from Sutton Bridge to King's Lynn had gone and water was spreading across all the fens as far inland as Ely and March. A coaster at Wisbech had been lifted bodily out of the river and dumped on the quay. The last train from Hunstanton to Kings Lynn had not got through. Dersingham had not seen her. She must be in the water somewhere near Heacham.

The surge swept south. Wells went next. Not much to worry about there. The Broads went in their turn. Almost simultaneously the great tract of land from Yarmouth to Reedham to Aldeby and Haddiscoe on to Beccles vanished. Harry Rampling, the District Superintendent, posed a problem. 'The last London stands outside Yarmouth South Town station. Water is running like a race under the M&GN Bridge. The line is cut behind her at Aldeby. Shall we call her in?' Well, long range decisions on safety are suicidal. I said: 'Can someone go and probe under the bridge?' 'No, it's running like a race.' 'Can someone get on the bridge above and probe from there?' 'No, it's too high.' There was nothing for it. 'Call her in' I said and heard half an hour later that she was home and dry. Two days later I went down to Yarmouth. Under the bridge was a crater four feet deep and about eleven feet wide. We had been very lucky indeed. Then another tale began to come out of Yarmouth. Inspector Anderson had taken a dinghy and had set off to rescue a panic-stricken signalman in Breydon Bridge signalbox half a mile out in the Broads. It transpired later that every ten strokes he had to stop and bale – and was blown back about the distance he had gained. He plugged on and with cracking muscles and after an aeon of time he was at the foot of the ladder. The signalman clambered aboard and with two of them they made better time going home. My boss, when he arrived in the morning, said: 'That was pretty good. Let the District write him a citation' and in due course Inspector Anderson got a BEM.

Aldeburgh was next. Station on high ground. The line was cut where it crossed the marsh. Next were Felixstowe and Harwich. High ground on both sides of a narrow estuary. So a violent storm which ships rode out – part of Felixstowe and most of Harwich were inundated. Clacton and Walton were on high ground but the Brightlingsea branch was swept away. Later the Crouch and Roach flooded thousands of acres around Southminster. The surge rolled on to Shoeburyness and Southend. It literally struck at Canvey Island with heavy loss of life.

Lastly came London. Our railways in the East End were in a low pocket; Blackwall Wharf, and Thames Wharf marshalling yard. The flood came with enormous suddenness. Ten feet of water within minutes. The staff had been warned but one Inspector had remained behind. The water rose to his shoulders when Providence sent him floating by a ladder. He got astride the ridge pole of a shunter's hut and prayed for the dawn. Then came the real blow. Barking Creek flooded Ilford – no Colchester line. The Lea burst and flooded Temple Mills Marshalling Yard, and the Cambridge Main Line round Tottenham. Then came the good news. The Hunstanton train was back in Hunstanton and the Railway Hotel ran rallying round with baths and breakfasts and makeshift clothing. They had run down the hill from Hunstanton and just beyond Heacham had met a wall of water with a bungalow on top. The bungalow had hit the vacuum pipe on the engine square on and torn it off. The water had put out the fire and risen to the level of the seats in the compartments. Guard Bruce had got the ten people including three children into one compartment. The children were put on the racks to sleep if possible. The rest Guard Bruce entertained with stories and conversation and even

Floods in March 1947 following the severe winter. This is Temple Mills yard well under water.

song – all standing on the seats of course. After four hours it seemed that the floods were subsiding, if slowly. In another hour Bruce took his emergency axe and chopped some dry wood off the brake van. With infinite care they lit a fire in the firebox and in something under an hour had enough steam to move. The water was still three feet deep. Bruce got out into it at the back of the train and, sounding with a pole as he went, piloted it back to dry land. Guard Bruce also got a BEM for his night's work.

When Alec Dunbar arrived we looked at our non-railway. We could not get into or out of London except to Enfield. We could run local trains on the high land, Bishops Stortford to Witham, Hertford to Buntingford if anyone wanted to go. All down the east side from Colchester to Wells, down the western side from Spalding to Kings Lynn and Spalding to March and Ely the fens were drowned – hundreds of square miles. We settled down to wait for doves with olive branches. One by one they came. Dan Rose, Yardmaster Temple Mills, went pushing and sounding on a pilot down the Cambridge line. In the afternoon he cleared it, warning that there was still two feet of water and timber from the furniture firms floating everywhere. Barking Creek had subsided so we had both main lines open.

Floods in February 1953. The high tides and easterly gales brought massive floods to much of the East Coast and Thames Estuary. The brunt of the damage was taken by Great Eastern section lines such as the Brightlingsea branch seen here.

Over the next week gradually the railway lines stood out like pencils above the water. Washouts were repaired. Whitemoor got going again to Norwich, Ipswich, Colchester and Temple Mills, northwards too of course.

It took over a fortnight for Thames Wharf to clear and more to restore the breaches and to get us railways in Broadline.

Everyone was caught. The Meteorological Office, the Coastguard, the Police, the railways. Looking back, Guard Bruce's train should never have left Hunstanton and we should have done much more to evacuate staff and rolling stock to high ground. The only permanent memorial is the Thames Barrage.

The whole thing brought us one benefit. The land was of course salt. It would not grow normal crops for maybe five years. We ran hundreds and hundreds of trains of gypsum from Nottinghamshire to the area around Southminster and to some of the fens.

But now, thinking years later, I was privileged to be in the middle of the greatest railway disaster of all time. 'Flooding' means now something quite different from hoses and fire brigades in my book.

ANY ANSWERS

In the years after the war we had a spate of people pulling communication cords; suburban trains mostly to Enfield or Chingford; boy also meets girl. The procedure was for the Operating Department which was understandably indignant at the damage to its punctuality and the duty to the people in the three or four following trains to apply to the Chief of Police for a prosecution. We got nowhere with this. Magistrates thought Norman Jasper's men were of full and merry habit who thought a turn-up with a girl in a train no more than anyone could expect and did not care a fig for our punctuality. The six hundred people in the trains behind could get on with it too if they had a mind. Eventually came a case which I thought even wall-eyed old Norman could not ignore. Between Bethnal Green and Cambridge Heath there descended from a window a scarf, a pullover, a bra and a roll-on. Then she rose like a rocket and pulled the cord. The Guard's report was in highly puritanical tone. I wrote in a state of high moral indignation to Norman once again, who once again said No and added that we must leave him to judge where to draw the line. I wrote back: 'In order to save further useless correspondence would he lay down as a principle whether he was going to draw the line above or below the belt.' Norman took this with the utmost gravity and reported me to my boss for the exercise of a Wiccanical sense of humour on serious subjects. And I suppose it was a serious subject. Certainly the punctuality was.

The second answer came when at about the same period we made a list of time lost by the Up Southend trains in the morning peak. L. P. Parker, the Locomotive Running Superintendent, replied in two lines: 'This phenomenon is not unconnected with the fall of the autumn leaf.' This I knew to be true because I kept the letters.

But from Stuart Ward the other day I find that it has turned itself into verse. Can anyone elucidate the mystery?

From G. F. Fiennes to L. P. Parker

> Your Southend trains are losing time
> A horrible crime
> To contrive to lose time .
> They struggle along hardly faster than I, Sir
> Have the farmers been spreading their spring fertiliser?
> They don't travel nearly as fast as they oughter
> Is it salt in the water?
> Or is it the fall of the autumnal leaf?
> Great Grief!

From L. P. Parker to G. F. Fiennes

> I am rather short of time
> So I rather fear my rhyme
> Will not compare with yours in ease and polish
> But I do so much agree
> That time lost by you and me
> Is a thing we ought to totally abolish.

October 1953

THE GLOOMY COMMUTER

'Who', said this chap on Wadhurst station to my brother Michael some ten years ago, 'Is that gloomy commuter with a name something like yours?' 'That' said Michael 'is my brother Gerry. He is gloomy for three principal reasons. We are a gloomy family. His wife has died. And he has just been appointed Chief Operating Officer of British Railways.'

'Then' said this chap, seizing on what seemed to him to be the important point 'we shall get a better service to Wadhurst.'

And as far as I remember it at least didn't get a lot worse, if indeed it altered at all.

But where the chap was wrong – and so was Bro' Mike – was in ascribing my expression to gloom rather than to a conscious effort to be serious on commuter trains.

We were taught on the LNER, which was not born to commuters, did nothing to achieve them but had Ilford, Romford, Becontree and Southend thrust upon it, that we had to treat commuters with deadly seriousness. There is nothing, so the LNER held, which converts a critic more surely into an implacable and unrelenting enemy than the idea that his letter for which he had dredged the dictionary for adjectives is read by the manager with merry laughter on his lips.

And more recently we had had the bitter example of a campaign waged by the Southend Travellers Association, which stemmed from the then railway manager at Fenchurch Street greeting the Association's secretary in the refreshment room, whereupon the secretary burst into tears and buried his head in his arms. 'Why' he sobbed 'do you never take me seriously?'

Billy Reynolds stayed him with cups of tea and fair words but the chap emigrated to Australia, leaving behind a bitter and twisted Association, which it took £25m spent on electrification to appease.

So when I got to the British Railways Board as Chief Operating Officer I took two steps, both subjective. I dealt with my expression and I changed the name. In a sense I couldn't have done the first without the second, because if, as we then did, we knew commuters, not as commuters but as 'Season Ticket Holders' and dealt with the Bishops Stortford Season Ticket Holders Association and the Sevenoaks Season Ticket Holders Association, I suffered internally and often from the small and reprehensible spring of laughter which associated them with 'the young lady of Staines, who loved to be ravaged in trains. She was given a season for no other reason by a man with more urges than brains.'

So, as befitted the serious subject and against who knows what departmental opposition season ticket holders became commuters, regardless of the fact that in a few years they would be all mixed up and mis-spelt.

'CHAOS AT LIVERPOOL STREET' was the poster of the evening paper, drawing on its limited vocabulary and referring to some small irregularity in the service, 'Our reporter found the stationmaster besieged by irate computers . . .'

When I went to an armchair at the British Railways Board there were none of these things to keep me amused. It was only a temporary substitute to reflect why doors would particularise in detail not only 'Ladies' and 'Gentlemen' but also 'for Members Only' and why so often a five star general lurked behind a door marked Private. So it was in my own commuting that things happened; and it was unsuitable that one morning this chap at Wadhurst of Bro' Michael's acquaintance who took such a gloomy view of me should be in my compartment.

He naturally with the rest opened *The Financial Times*. I as I always do, because it is the best and maybe the only time of day to do so, began to work and because it was a useful demonstration to those who claimed that they can neither read nor write in a Hastings diesel set that they have been doing the first and that I was doing the second. Brother Michael himself needs some correction on these points and gets it from that stout champion of BR, my wife Jean – sorry, more correction, for 'stout' read 'strong'.

We went quickly and reasonably smoothly on our way to the approaches of London Bridge. Then, there was a slight sort of hiccup in the forward rush, which made me put down my work and attend. The brakes went on and we came to a stand. On the other five tracks trains rushed by, some one way, some the other. We remained silent, too silent. The engines had shut down.

Soon the chap said 'We often wait here. They have to get one out before we get in'. At any given moment in the London morning peak there are six people in the approaches to Paddington, Euston, King's Cross, St Pancras, Liverpool Street and Victoria saying those words. And often they are true.

Not this time. Train after train rushed by out of London, clearing vast numbers of platforms for us. A silent weight of public opinion began to build up and press down on the corner

The concourse at Liverpool Street east side after electrification to Southend Victoria in 1956. The peak hour service was so frequent that if passengers missed one train there was another in a few minutes. (*British Railways*)

where I sat. I began to wish two things, firstly for the Spitalfield Pilot whose time for this sort of rescue was a par seventeen minutes and I regretted that I had done so much to abolish it, although less than the firebug who handed it its redundancy notice by burning Bishopsgate Goods.

Secondly I wished I was the great and good Doctor Beeching; not for his brain because he worked far too hard for one as workshy as myself, nor for his tastes because he drank gin before meals while I am a winebiber, but for his capacity to handle commuters eyeball to eyeball.

'I got this train here to time to-day' he once told a compartment, 'By sheer will-power. Let's see for the rest of the week what you lot can do.'

My efforts in that sort of line have been self-defeating. Once, later on, I was travelling from Maidenhead to London with George Gibb, later Mr Freightliner.

George said 'There's a rumour going around, Gerry, that you are going to make the Paddington commuter service pay.'

And I said, in my simple error, very earnestly, 'Yes, George, and there's only one way to make it pay. Make them sit closer together, Make some of them stand.'

The four *Financial Times* in the four corners came slowly and simultaneously down from before four faces – eight eyes made sure that they would know me again. *The Times* went up. None of them said a word but within a month they had formed a Protection Association which defeated half the plan to make them pay for their ride. Maybe they were right because now the Paddington service has a splendid subsidy out of which the commuters get their luxury service and out of which BR make a profit. All are pleased. The only dissatisfied bloke is me living in Suffolk and contributing to Henley through my income tax. Still, they contribute to my East Suffolk line through theirs. So maybe we should all be delighted. Maybe . . .

In this Hastings diesel in the approaches to London Bridge one of the absent emotions was delight. Nor was it apparent when very rightly the Guard appeared. He was as many of the Southern guards are, a version of Sunny South Sam. He beamed largely and universally on us and brought us his idea of good news.

'The engines have failed' he said, 'we shall be here some time.'

As so often, the idea that anybody on British Railways firstly knows what is happening and secondly passes on the knowledge to his passengers struck this compartment spellbound. Long before anyone spoke we could hear Sam far down the corridor bringing his glad tidings to others.

So when anyone did speak it was of course the chap from Wadhurst and it was to me he spoke.

'The engines have failed, have they?' he said. 'Here some time, huh! Why have they failed and how long are we to be here?'

The essence of this situation is firmness. A week or so ago on the 12.30 from Liverpool Street there came into our compartment René Cutforth, fresh from a triumph at Broadcasting House and fresh from having to stand in a queue, which among other things at Liverpool Street he thought was awful.

'There is nothing awful about Liverpool Street' I said at dictation speed.

Jean, who was in the seat between us shrank visibly into her skin as she does when I act like this. Sometime I must tell you how in the Gare d'Austerlitz I was shaken like a rat by the enquiry clerk so she has some justification. Firmness doesn't always work; but on this night we had a most agreeable journey to Witham where to my sorrow he got out.

So in the approaches to London Bridge and knowing that I would have to disguise the passage of quite a lot of time, because I was sure there was no Spitalfields pilot and the Southern Region par for this course would be more like a golf than seventeen minutes I began:

'There are forty-three separate failures in the book of instruction which can happen and have happened to a diesel engine – and a lot more that no one has yet thought of, of which this may be one. All the driver knows at this moment is that all systems are no-go. He has said to himself and to his guard the mystic and pregnant words 'No amps'. He has pressed the starter button four times the number of times which the instructions say he should have pressed it. He has still no amps. He is now checking whether this is one of the six failures that he can recognise and is allowed to remedy. If it is not – and the odds are that is is not – he will either send for a fitter or for a second train to push us along.

'Can you' said the chap 'recognise more than six failures?'

'No' I said shortly. As a friend on the Central Electricity Board said to me once 'For me electricity is something which I can't see, I can't hear, I can't smell and daren't touch.' No amps for me. The only method by which I once got a failed electric train going was by kicking it sharply. The doors which had stuck open closed and off we went. In passing I suspect that many other families also live on the principle of 'Wait till dadda gets home and he will give it a bang.'

'The trains never failed', said a new and welcome voice, 'when we had steam engines.'

There must be – somewhere between heaven and hell – a Hall of Repentance for the people who say this and the two other things; firstly 'Before the war all trains ran to time' and secondly 'of course British Railways are running down the line with the object of closing it'.

Here I had to nail only one of these splendid mendacities and take a nice long time to do so.

I said 'Out of the many spectacular failures of steam engines in commuter service in which I have been a participant let me select one. It greatly offended at the time the Southend Travellers Association aforesaid because the basic cause was nothing mechancial for which they could blame BR but was a shortage of water. And Southend has gone to great expense to surround itself with water – on the sea side salt, which once in a hundred years overflows the sea walls into Canvey Island which is outside the Borough and therefore irrelevant and twice a day gradually approaches the esplanade thereby justifying the title Southend on Sea. On the shore side it has built splendid reservoirs which supplied the engines at Shoeburyness and Pitsea with the raw material for steam. On this occasion it failed.

The upshot of the whole brouhaha was that the station announcers at Fenchurch Street told the commuters in BR's soothing style 'a train has become derailed at Pitsea'. BR never derails a train; it becomes derailed; and if you can think of a better turn of phrase for this event let them – or indeed me – know.

Now the drill when the line via Upminster is blocked at Pitsea is to divert the trains to Southend at Upminster via Ockendon and Tilbury which costs them around fifteen minutes extra. It is all well understood. The engines were permitted to run by the alternate route. The drivers and the guards know the road. And the only people whom it enrages are those who travel one to a motor car and spend an unusual time standing at level crossings to watch the extra trains go by.

The executive order for the trains to run by the alternative route is given by the Railway Operating Control at Fenchurch Street. One touch of a switch brings the signalman at Upminster Junction to the phone.

'Off the road at Pitsea, everything via Ockendon.'

That is all. Then control gets on with telling the station inspectors at Upminster, Barking, and Fenchurch Street so that the drivers guards and passengers know what to expect, and lastly the signalmen at Ockendon, Grays, Tilbury and the rest.

Meantime the Chief Controller will be arranging to clear up the mess himself; getting out the accident vans and spare engines, district inspector and if it is more than a minor event informing his superintendent, engineer and public relations officer.

On this occasion, thanks to some brain storm – railway controls are known to the outside staff affectionately as 'the brains' – the Brains got its priorities wrong. Before the order went to Upminster Junction four trains had gone serenely on their way up the spout toward Pitsea on the line which was blocked by what had become derailed.

The Brains thought then like lightning. These trains must turn at Laindon, come back to Upminster, turn again and run via Ockendon. 'Hell' thought the Brains 'the engines won't have enough water for that. There is no water column at Laindon. We must,' thinking now with sheer brilliance, 'call out the fire brigade.'

When you call out the fire brigade and it is a railway occasion you get the full treatment. More than one engine; reflecting the rays of the sun from red paint and gleaming brass with more than oriental splendour; full crews in complete oilskins, crowned with gleaming crested helmets; several hundred yards of hose, and of course the end product, water.

They roared up the station approach, leaped from front, sides and back to the ground, demanded where was the fire, were not in the least dismayed by being asked to fill up four railway engines, rolled out the hoses in competition time and came to an abrupt and very sheepish halt. They had not brought the right adaptors to join the various lengths of hose.

One of our drivers said 'My bleeding oath . . . well, if you can't fill the tanks of these here four engines you have got four fires on your hands – in the fireboxes; and four explosions if you don't do something quick.'

In terms of self help there are nothing like natural forces. 'And' said the vicar at the parochial church council, congratulating the members on putting out a fire in the church hall 'All glory to Miss Tompkins who for two hours without pause passed water in a bucket.' We could have done with a dozen of her.

But it seemed that fires in fireboxes were railway work. So four weary railway firemen took their long handled shovels in hand and did what they knew how to do from previous failures on steam engines. They threw out the fires on to the permanent way. And five thousand stranded commuters who were no longer all that amused went home from Laindon by bus.'

There was in that compartment in the approaches to London Bridge a notable silence. It was broken by a slight jolt from the rear and we were in movement. I looked at my watch. I no longer regretted the Spitalfields pilot. I put all my other stories of steam failures away. We had been at a stand just seventeen minutes. There is a lot to be said for the Southern Region after all.

5

Whipping the Western

STEAM INTO DIESEL: I

You might have thought that the Western Region was the last place where diesels would be accepted in place of steam. And it was true that many depots kept some Kings and Castles and Halls in Great Western condition and ran them like cockbirds. On the other hand where there were diesels there was doubt and suspicion. Often a conversation like this took place:

'What does the speedo show?'

'83.'

'What is the limit?'

'90'.

'Well – come on – give her a bit more.'

'Well, we may get a failure.'

'If we do that's not your fault. If the nuts and bolts fall off that's up to the shed.'

And gradually they got going – so much so that one day, as the new General Manager, I was going down to South Wales. At Swindon the rush and clatter sounded impressive.

We were eleven minutes early. So at Newport I got out to tell the driver what a good guy he was. Now when you get on a footplate you greet the driver, flash your engine pass at him and settle down. He said: 'They tell me the new General Manager is on the train.'

I said: 'Well he was but he got out at Newport.'

D–I–D–0–0, he should have gone on to Cardiff. I wonder where the silly b's got to.'

'Here.'

And being a Welshman he collapsed with laughter.

113

STEAM INTO DIESEL: II

When we started our campaign to induce drivers to run diesels to the limit I had issued a bulletin saying that many men were driving to the line limits but too many were not giving us those last few miles an hour, and so on.

This produced a diatribe about denigrating the profession of drivers from a well-known firebrand at Landore, Trevor Curtis. I pondered over this and eventually wrote: 'If I say that Judas Iscariot was not so good an apostle am I denigrating the profession of apostles?'

The next thing that happened a couple of weeks later was Ena: 'I've got a Mr Curtis and his wife outside. . . .' We had an hour together and parted such firm buddies that when in 1967 I vanished from the railway scene like a puff of smoke Trevor went and chained himself to the railings of Downing Street on my behalf, bless him. There is glory for you.

SPEED

I have always been an apostle of speed. The timetables for the Shenfield electrification, for the Britannias, for the Deltics were designed to make the most of the power of the locomotive. And speed is something railways can sell. Now with the Inter-City 125 HSTs off at an average of 85–90 miles an hour or more we are beyond the range of competition from a sufficient market or the road.

Nevertheless let me repeat that the marketing side is not what it is all about. We are paid by the passenger mile. What is important is the number of passenger miles a diagram will collect.

So: Liverpool Street to Shenfield (persons) (peak)

	8 journeys × 1000 people	80,000
Britannias	450 miles × 200	90,000
Kings Cross to Leeds	376 miles × 200	75,250

But once – and it shows how insidious the Western can be – the showman prevailed over the railwayman. I had been nagging J. F. (Freddie) Harrison for 4000 horse power with no result. So after a while I said: 'Let's have a trial to Plymouth with double-headed English Electric 1750s.' So on Friday 4 June we set off at 8.28 with Inspector Bill Andress, Drivers Rees and Williams on the front. Aboard the train was a lot of Paddington, some from Liverpool Street, David Haliburton and his timing lads, the Oxford University Railway Society and Press, David St. John Thomas, Stuart Friend, and C. J. Allen. Some of the Old Pals Act. An exhilarating run. Reading 29 minutes, Newbury 44, Plymouth spot on three hours. 74.666 miles an hour. And in the 1950s I had said to the Railway Students Association that the Vitesse Commerciale is 75 miles an hour. We came back via Bristol in only 8 minutes more. 84 minutes from Bristol to London. Very impressive. I could see C. J. Allen logging the records. But the effective commercial return was about half that of Shenfield or Britannias.

So speed yes, but let there be money in it.

PERFORMANCE

Before the war the Great Western had a towering reputation for its passenger service. In safety, speed, punctuality, courtesy, comfort and profitability it was the tops. And indeed only part of the reputation was thanks to its publicity department which was undeniably also the tops. Much of it was true. After the war, after nationalisation, alas – the going was not so good. Indeed I recommend dyed-in-the-wool Western fans to skip this chapter. It gives the facts of a rapid decline under Western management and Western equipment which was only reversed when – and because – foreign managers were brought in and new equipment took over.

Safety first. In the lowest accident rates between 1948 and 1965 the Western Region appeared sixteen times, the best region of any. Two accidents only will appear in the histories and one of those will be for laughs. The serious one was at Milton in 1955 when a passenger train diverted from its normal route owing to engineering work crossed from main to loop at a high speed and went down an embankment. Eleven people were killed and 157 injured. A bad one. The driver claimed that the Automatic Warning System had not operated at the distant signal in rear. And that claim diverted some attention from his failure to observe the signal itself. The second accident in which four people only were injured occurred in 1951 outside Fishguard. An auto train left without the token for the single line. The signalman promptly got three detonators down in its path. He had a freight train coming. *But* there was a wedding party aboard. And the crack of the three legitimate detonators was lost in the general *feu de joie*, from the dozens which the fireman had been strewing around when he should have been collecting the token. The auto and the freight collided head-on with the result aforesaid. I remember a similar *feu de joie* after the wedding of Bill Johnson (later Sir Henry), Chairman of BRB and his Maisie. The moral is not that we should not have fun in our work but that at least one of us should be taking care while we do.

So far so good. Nevertheless, whereas the Great Western in the year before nationalisation was top of the league in safety, by 1965 the Western Region was in third or fourth place. Let us be fair; the change was due to a more rapid improvement by the other Regions. The Western was also significantly better – indeed good.

In speed the Great Western always enjoyed knocking hell out of the other railways. And very well it did it. Brunel started it on the Broad Gauge. Daniel Gooch abetted and followed him. Churchward made the great leap forward on which Collett built. Between the wars the Castles of the Great Western were supreme. The policy was the steam spectacular; to have the fastest train in the world, then the fastest train in Britain. The discrepancy between the fastest and the average was considerable. In August 1972 C. J. Allen quoted in *Modern Railways* the times for 1939 (*see table*).

Of the six principal services out of Paddington four averaged below 50 mph. The Great Western was *in fact* on average slower than the LNER or the LMS. Oh dear!

	Fastest	*Average*	*Difference*
	h m	h m	h m
Paddington–Bristol	1.45	2.18	0.33
Paddington–Cardiff	2.37	2.55	0.18
Paddington–Exeter	2.50	3.21	0.31
Paddington–Plymouth	4.00	5.41½	1.41½

That is water long under the bridge. What faced the Western Region after nationalisation was that competition from the motor car in speed and from the express coach in cost would intensify year by year; and that the competition would shrug off with insolent ease a challenge from a railway with one spectacular train each way a day. The challenge had to be based on a whole service. The Western had its problems. The locomotives had not come too well out of their now long service. Locomotive coal was poor. The design of the Castles and Kings, supreme between the wars, had not marched forward in the same way as Gresley and Stanier had marched. However, the real problem was one of attitude. The managers still hankered for the steam spectacular. In contrast with the period after the Kaiser's war when the first even-time departure timetable in the country appeared at Paddington as quickly as 1922, it was nine years after the end of the war in 1954 when the Bristolian reappeared with a time of 105 minutes, worked mainly by Castles with the re-designed superheaters and streamlined steam passages. No amount of hankering by the management or pressure by the faithful or individual runs in as little as 92 minutes could convince the locomotive department that a timing of 100 minutes could be written into a timetable. So the blue riband of speed went wandering around the East Coast, on the Great Northern, then believe it or not on the Great Eastern and in the final years of steam traction on the North Eastern. In 1959 the 2200hp Warship diesels were entrusted with the 100 minute timing; but as I have written elsewhere we needed at least 3000 horsepower under the bonnet. They were not masters of the job. They rode shockingly at high speeds, lurching and driving and banging; so in 1960 back to 105 minutes and in 1961 even more. However, in 1961 the 2700hp D1000 class were around and cut the time to 105. It was not until 1971 that the Western achieved 100 minutes permanently. And it goes to show how Westernised I have become that I have written on and on about a 'spectacular' in which as a policy I strongly disbelieve.

So in 1960 on a visit from BRB Headquarters to the Lecture and Debating Society at Cardiff, back to the truth. 'You in Cardiff are 145 miles from London. The average time of your day-time expresses is 3 hours 3 minutes, 48 miles an hour. Your passengers, take door to door 3½ to 4 hours. When the Severn Bridge and the Western Motorway are built the car owner will be in the West End of London in just over three hours. If you choose to compete for speed you must get to Paddington in two hours – 73 mph. And why not?'

The general improvement in the service had to await the 2700hp diesels. By 1961 the Western had over 400 main line diesels and over 700 two years later. What the Great Western had done in 1922 the Western Region did between 1961 and 1965. It overhauled its express passenger timetable completely.

It was not an easy task. We had, firstly, an administrative problem. Our divisions did the timing, co-ordinated by meetings at Regional Headquarters. Now we manage a railway most efficiently when the two terminals of a service are under one manager. So should be Paddington on the one hand and Plymouth, Bristol, Swansea and Worcester on the other. Therefore we centralised timing and diagramming, with, let it be said, very little difference of opinion. The centralisation, let it be said also and quietly, made it much easier to forget the single 'spectacular' and to design a service in which all trains would be spectacular in terms of competition with the coach and with the car.

That problem was the easy one. The difficult one was how far could we trust, how hard could we push our new diesels. In 1963 we had in the top class 74 D1000's of 27000hp to take the place of 30 Kings and 171 Castles. One of the highlights in my career was the weeks during which Assistant General Manager Tommy Mathewson-Dick and I allowed the D1000s to continue in service knowing that one had derailed itself with an axle fractured from metal fatigue. We got to within a hair of grounding our express passenger fleet. If this was the worst, it was by no means the only 'Bug'. The actual availability of the class for traffic varied from day to day between 40 and 60 per cent. And if anyone tells me that the figures published showed around 80 per cent, I agree. So they did. And if anybody tells me to design a timetable on the basis of a locomotive being declared 'available for traffic' if it is so available for one hour in 24, then I shall stop having been a timetable clerk.

For timetabling therefore we could rely on only 35 of our 74 D1000s. Until 1965 when the Brush 2750hp class came along in numbers – and by then the D1000s were cured of many of their ills – our replacement for 2700hp were the 2000hp Warship Class, the 1700hp Hymeks and the remaining steam Kings and Castles. None of these were capable of competing with the car.

Therefore we had to advance slowly. Luckily our geography helped us. Unlike the East Coast and the West Coast main lines which have a long single spine – on the East Coast for 156 miles to Doncaster – the Western has a split only a little over 30 miles out at Reading for Devon and Cornwall and another some 85 miles out at Wootton Bassett for Bath and Bristol, South Wales. We could divide the service into three major parts and accelerate each in turn as the locomotives became in truth available.

Not only available but predictable. It is one of the advances which diesel and electric traction, particularly electric, have brought to a manager that he can say to a designer: 'Produce me a locomotive which will haul x tons from A to B over such-and-such conditions of track in y minutes.' And from the drawing board he can receive standard times. The trial runs, of which we did a number, were partly because we did not entirely believe the designer, but largely for show.

Elsewhere, I have told the story of a diesel trip to Plymouth to forestall a steam specacular by setting a target. It had however also a serious object, to confirm the calculations

The new order on the Western Region when one of the first diesel-electric locomotives of the Brush class 47 was named *North Star* on 20 March 1965 and then worked a special train to Bristol. Until then the Western's diesel fleet had consisted uniquely on BR of diesel-hydraulic types of German origin. But the Western had to be made to conform.

from a drawing board. Out of these efforts came a schedule of standard times for the D1000s and Brush 2750hp (now Class 47 to you). At 84½ minutes 75.4mph for the 107 miles to Bath and 98, 72.5mph, for 118 to Bristol with 465 tons; not bad. But to that we had to add something for the Civil Engineer's temporary speed restrictions. Although with new techniques the track was in theory 'Fit and Forget' and although the Civils were much more self-disciplined (or, anyway, disciplined) about track possessions in express hours than of old, we thought we had to add five minutes for him. So we were back to 100 minutes or so to Bristol.

And of course back to my own knowledge that we needed not 2700hp but over 3000hp under the bonnet. We tried to borrow a Deltic for trials but the 'Rude Mechanicals' were unaccountably shy. So we went out on 16 June 1965 behind two 1750hp diesels. We had from the Civils permission for 100mph; we had from the Mechanicals authority to over-speed the 90mph Type 3's until the overspeed trip cut us out. With Chief Inspector Andress and Driver Reg Williams in the front cab and with the BR prototype train XP64 trailing, off we went. Seven minutes to Ealing paid due regard to shaking the immemorial dust of Paddington off our feet and 98mph through Slough and Maidenhead was heartening. Then came the long drag through the valley of the Kennet with its intolerable speed restrictions. Once I was on the footplate with Smitherman and sounding off about the chap, not Brunel, who with a wide valley along which to lay a railway swung it from side to side crossing the river by a right angle bridge each time the two met.

'I suppose' I said, 'he couldn't design a skew bridge.'

'I'd always heard' said Smitherman, 'that he got paid by the mile.'

However very precise driving up to but not beyond the limits of the thirteen permanent restrictions between Reading and Taunton gained us eight minutes and to Exeter nine minutes ahead of the 1964 trial with D1027. At Exeter in 132 minutes we had run a record at 78.7mph. Up 3500 horsepower. Then we plugged round the curves and hammered up the hills to Plymouth, 225 miles in all in 196 minutes. We had shown that timings of 2½ hours to Exeter and 3½ hours to Plymouth were reasonable bets in a timetable with 3500hp under the bonnet.

Homewards, Tom Rees drove. We came back via Bristol and Badminton. In 1904 *City of Truro* ran Plymouth to Bristol in 120 min. We did no better – in fact a few seconds more. Knowing how we swung round the curves and being told how *City of Truro* was over seven minutes faster between Plymouth and Newton Abbot, it was clear that anyone on the train in 1904 had exchanged seasickness for the sensations of a full gale on land. For all that from Exeter to Bristol, 75 miles in 58 minutes, was what we had set out to demonstrate. After that the record of 87 minutes to Paddington via Badminton was standard stuff, even if we spent a lot of time at 100mph with the overspeed trip behaving admirably from our point of view.

What was the only disagreeable conclusion was the inference to be drawn from having taken 196 minutes down via Westbury and only nine minutes more homewards via Bristol. Is it worth maintaining to express standards the hundred miles between Reading and Taunton or should, as James Ness unsuccessfully argued, the West Country expresses run via Bristol? I had already answered that question in favour of keeping the Westbury route and now shuffled it under the rug.

This has been a long story about managers' decisions. Translation into timetables brought a letter in April 1965 from Cecil J. Allen comparing the service in 1965/66 with 1939, the 'steam spectacular' with the 'standard service'. We had not gone all the way. The Bristolian in 1939 was five minutes faster than our standard. So was the fastest train to Worcester. But we were timing to Exeter in 2 hours 33 against 2 hours 50 and to Cardiff in 2 hours against 2 hours 37, and so on. And of course we had fully or nearly an hourly frequency. 'This' he wrote, 'is a fine record of achievement on which you and your staff are very warmly to be congratulated and to many of us it is very pleasant indeed to see the "Great

Western" getting back to its former position in the front rank of British Railway speed. And I know that you have not finished yet.'

We were in fact winning. The number of passengers had stopped declining and was moving strongly upward. No direct comparisons were possible owing to the changes in the boundaries of the Region but on a fair estimate, 112m in 1948 had declined to 104m in 1960 and recovered to 110m in 1965.

Punctuality was also a story of success up to a point. No figure looks good when one quotes a full year. For one thing the timetables do not time trains with full recovery allowances in the winter for the extra rolling resistances, long hours of darkness, slower moving passengers and slower moving staff. So let it not come as a shock that the percentage of express trains to time on the Western Region in 1948 was 22; by 1955 it was no better than 25 per cent but in 1962 there came a lift from 36 to 48 per cent and in 1964 52 per cent. No wonder no one was keen to accelerate services between 1948 and 1961, that is before the diesels arrived in numbers. In 1963 and 1964 we had a lot of fun. By then we had some 750 main-line diesels and I didn't see why we should be bumping around near the bottom of the punctuality league.

We set out to teach homo sapiens erectus railwayanus to abandon his casual habits and to run trains to time. The first task was with ourselves. Will officers kindly instruct their stations that trains will no longer wait for passengers strolling down the hill or from one platform to another? Will officers kindly instruct their controls not to stop trains where they are not booked to stop for anyone except the Sovereign? Will officers no longer stop trains for themselves? Will the engineers kindly keep off the fast lines during 'express' hours? Will officers get out and about and encourage louder whistles, more noisy slamming of doors, more dramatic waving of flags? And they did.

The other principal task was with the most important man on the railway, the driver. A diesel was like a first watch to a boy. He treats it like an egg in case it comes apart in his hands. And of course the diesels often did come apart in their hands.

The locomotive inspectors were straitly charged to tell drivers to run to time – or to make up time, if late – and if the nuts and bolts fell off, then it would be not the drivers' fault but ours. Finally we charged the mechanical engineers to see that the nuts and bolts did not fall off. And in the winter of 1963/64 away we went.

In January 1964 we had the best result ever achieved by the Western Region, 55.7 per cent; and we were second in the league. In February we were top with 68.2 per cent, the second best figure ever recorded in February by any Region. In June we had 73.7 per cent, the best ever for the Region in any month. At that stage I invited to the Aldwych Brasserie a mixed blessing of drivers, guards, fitters, inspectors and managers. We had a memorable evening. I blessed them in a memorable speech. They laughed themselves sick. We kept it up for three more months. But by October we were back to fifth in the league. However, the worst figure for any month was 54.7 per cent; and in December with 56.4 we were back to second. I am not sure what the moral of this is. Three things are for sure. The first is that homo sapiens and all that is a casual, unpunctual character; the second is that you have to keep after him all the time; the third is that it is no way to make him deny that character by doing as British Railways now do, namely to give him an alibi by quoting their figures of punctuality as 'trains up to five minutes late'.

Now, reluctantly, to the nitty-gritty – money – and some odious comparisons. I do not pretend that the figures are the outcome of a Profit and Loss Account. Taking one Region with another however and one year with another they provide a fair judgment. So:

Surplus or deficit £m	Western	Eastern
1948	+0.6	+1.5
1953	—	+8.1
1958	−20.0	—
1961	−30.0	−1.0
1963	−16.0	+2.0
1964	−11.0	+3.5
1965	−6.0	+6.0

This plunge into deficit poses questions – especially as the Western was accompanied only by the LM. On the whole the Eastern, Southern and North Eastern held the line. The Scottish had never had a good out turn anyway. The first question is easily answered. The fault was not in receipts. The two Regions were about level in 1948. Still level in 1958 and give or take the transfer of Birmingham, level in 1964. But on the expenditure side:

Expenses £m	Western	Eastern
1948	54	55
1953	72	64
1958	107	85
1948/58 Increase	53	30

Nor was the difference in geography. The Western in 1950 had 36 fewer route miles than in 1948; the Eastern 226. Alas the difference was in performance. The Eastern carried 78m more passengers and 4m tons more freight with 22,000 less staff. The Western carried no more passengers and 3m tons less freight with 2,000 less staff. In the speed of passenger trains the Western had gone to the bottom of the table; of freight trains from third to fourth, while the Eastern had gone from sixth to third. In the overall efficiency of freight movement, net ton miles per train engine hour, the Western had sunk from first to fifth; the Eastern had risen from third to first. A census in 1950 showed the staff costs for enginemen and guards per train mile to be the highest of any Region. And so on.

Nowadays, maybe, someone would have bleated 'This is all the Government's fault' and sat on his hands. Not so the Great and Good Doctor. He concluded that it was the fault of the Western's managers. And between 1960 and 1962 there was something like a clean sweep through Paddington. That is the subject of the next chapter. For the moment it is relevant only to say that in the next years the number of staff was cut from 113,000 to 49,000 and the deficit from a high point of £30m in 1961 to £6m in 1965. In the two years 1964 and 1965 the productivity of the staff as measured by units handled per man went up from 1,600 to over 2,300 or by over 40 per cent.

THE LAND BEYOND THE TAMAR

In October 1963 Cornwall was not very pleased with its railway managers. They foresaw the closure of almost all their branch lines under the Beeching Reshaping Report, just published. And they gave entire credence to a rumour that the malignant management was to close all railways west of Devonport by the simple device of declaring Brunel's Royal Albert Bridge at Saltash unsafe for traffic. There was also a reporter on *The Western Morning News*, David St John Thomas, who had a habit of correcting – and rightly correcting – the hand-outs from our public relations department. The Divisional Manager, David Pattison was having a thin time.

So I betook myself to Plymouth. The first priority was this St John Thomas. In five minutes I knew I need not have bothered. He was not an 'investigative journalist'; he was someone like me who had been bitten by the bug of railways and wished passionately for their success. Action needed – tell him the truth.

Stage two was a dinner for the local MPs. They were a strong and highly entertaining lot. Dame Joan Vickers, Sir Doublas Marshall, Jeremy Thorpe, Peter Mills, Greville Howard and a most formidable Chairman of the County Council, Alderman Foster. I made my usual response to the malignancy and closure plans. A railway manager likes managing railways. The more railway he manages, the higher his salary and the more impressive his status . . . and so on. Then I had an inspiration. As rumours arise from who knows where and from what reason so can they be blown away just as easily. I said to Dame Joan Vickers: 'Will you go up into the overhead tube of the Saltash Bridge tomorrow with an engineer? We will run some trains underneath and you tell us if it is safe or unsafe?' She made no bones about it. All she said

The key to Cornwall – the Royal Albert Bridge between Saltash and Devonport linking Cornwall with the rest of the BR network. The much later road bridge is on the left. Gerry Fiennes once persuaded local MP Dame Joan Vickers to climb through the suspension tubes to see for herself how good the bridge was and killed off rumours that BR was using the condition of the bridge to close the railway into Cornwall.

was: 'May I wear my trousers?' Next day up she went – a forty foot vertical ladder with the Assistant District Engineer behind her. We ran the trains. She came down. 'The rock of Gibraltar will fall down before the Saltash Bridge does.' End of rumour. End of campaign.

Mawes, Germane, Mawgan, Gwythian, Ives, Erth. All Cornish saints although they don't appear in our reference books. Dreary fellows you would think. But to one, if I had been a Catholic, I would have lit candles in 1964. We broke the law and against all reason we prevailed. It can only have been that warrior saint, St Blazey. After Saltash I went around Cornwall looking for its salvation, not on the passenger side but on the freight. And soon I came to St Blazey, the centre of the china clay trade. The china clay went either for export in big ships from our own port at Fowey or coastwise from either Fowey or the English China Clay company's port at Par nearby.

The system, as planned, was a good one. The companies washed the clay out of the hills into sluices which led to settling ponds called 'Dries'. When a ship was nearly due the clay was dug out into wagons, taken to Fowey or Par, shipped and gone. So why, oh why, was every siding for miles around full of loaded wagons? The answer was at Fowey and no doubt Par also. The unbelievable inefficiency of coastwise shipping. Ships not arriving according to their ETA (Estimated time of arrival) messages. Ships arriving dirty and spending twenty-four to forty-eight hours cleaning. Ships needing repair.

So Paddington did a pilot scheme for trains direct from the Dries to the paper mills in Kent. They reported that allowing ourselves a handsome profit we could undercut coastwise shipping by shillings a ton. But when I said 'Go ahead' they replied: 'Well, there is the law.' And it was true that coastwise shipping was protected from undercutting by railways. Now the inspiration from Paddington – or it may have been St Blazey at my shoulder, – made me say: 'At Fowey and at Par eight out of ten ships which I saw were German or Dutch or Belgian or French. Whom is this law protecting? Let us break it.'

When the contract was signed we had a symposium of the MPs. They were highly diverted. They did not promise any public support but that they would tread the corridors of power on our behalf.

The trains began to run – most successfully. St Blazey was delighted with its new fleet of 2–8–0s and with being taught the road to Exeter. Then the first blow fell. The Under-Secretary for Transport, Vice Admiral Hughes Hallett nailed the masthead – if there is a mast-head in the House of Commons. 'How' he bellowed 'shall we take the next British Army off the beaches of Dunkirk if the railways are allowed to massacre our coastwise shipping?' The next blow followed

Gerry Fiennes presides over the naming of another Class 47 *City of Truro* and presents a painting of the GWR 4–4–0 of that name and the BR Class 47 to the Mayor of Truro.

softly – an instruction from the Ministry to raise our rates to those of coastal shipping. At Paddington we were cast down – unnecessarily because the papermakers said: 'The new service is so good that we will pay the higher rate.'

Soon after – query St Blazey again – John Peyton became Minister of Transport. The Vice-Admiral reverted to the back benches. One day I was expounding to John that Cornwall could not afford three forms of transport, road, rail and coastwise; and that I was planning clay liners to the potteries and to grab the coastwise power station coal to Hayle and the domestic coal to Padstow and so on. John did not demur. So I said: 'The next broadside from the Vice Admiral will blow us out of the water.' John, who was a quiet man but an excellent minister said: 'Remember the Admiral only fires blanks now.'

Cornwall in 1964, to sum it up, was now friendly territory. David St John Thomas and *The Western Morning News*, the members of Parliament, the County Council were actively supporting us. The Saltash Bridge, so said Dame Joan Vickers, was not going to fall down. Clay liner trains were running to Kent and to the Potteries. The coal for Hayle Power Station was on rail. P. G. Wodehouse used to warn the smog by saying that round the next corner there is a man with a sandbag. So it proved. In 1965 the great and good Doctor issued 'The Red Peril'. Lines for investment and development were shewn in red. Lines where no investment should take place and should wither on the stem were in grey. The whole of Cornwall was grey.

Paddington's response – and remember that they had been on a high diet of oats – was to order for St Blazey a new fleet of clay liner wagons and diesels of the largest size. They were put on early programmes of investment. Indeed within a few years the HST 125s were running through to Penzance.

Will someone who reads this – say General Manager Sidney Newby – do the honours to St Blazey; say name a locomotive after him on which he rides on a white charger with helm and shield and lance. The last should be lowered in the direction of Whitehall.

WESTERN

To: Station Manager
Paddington

From: General Manager
Paddington
1.4.65

I was struck all of a heap yesterday by seeing a Ticket Collector at Reading with a carnation in his buttonhole. It gave such a tone to the whole proceedings that I wonder if we cannot extend the practice to Paddington station and get volunteers to bring to the office during the holiday season a few roses, carnations, or what-have-you from their gardens, so that we could brighten up Paddington.

I would certainly do this as long and as often as I remembered.

WOMEN!

On Thursday, 2 February 1965 I had one of those days which Ena had been strictly commanded to mark 'Keep Clear' in the diary. This used to be referred to by the Chairman in tones of dreadful scorn as 'swanning around.' I do not know what the justification was. I had fun. Some of the staff saw the Old Man and got off their chests what was on them. And of course the grapevine spread anything good like 'I wonder where the silly b——'s got to' which gave a sense of reality to a shadowy figure at Paddington. Anyway, once a fortnight we kept a clear day.

On this day I went down to Swindon, changed on to the footplate of a 'Gloucester.' The crew was so animated about the run-down in Swindon works that they were almost too late at throwing out the anchors and to stop at a level crossing. On this crossing were two large women, tugging without hope of success at an enormous, recalcitrant dog. There was no sign of the crossing keeper. The crew was beginning to get down and join in the tug-a-dog. I said: 'He doesn't know you. You'll get bitten. Try the cylinder-cocks'. So we shouted to the women to stand clear. We crawled forward with the cocks open. The dog looked at us with contempt. Suddenly he took the hedge with a leap like Arkle and was streaking across the field like a scalded cat.

At Gloucester across our bow ran a freight, a Washwood Heath to Severn Tunnel Junction. I clambered up into the brake van. No guard. Soon he arrived, gave the Right Away. Then I said in due form: 'Fiennes, General Manager, Paddington.' He said: 'Banup, Goods Guard, secretary of the Maesglas LDC (Local Departmental Committee). I said: 'I've heard of you. You are the most awkward chap on the Western Region.' The lads never seem to mind what you say to them. We had a couple of hours to Severn Tunnel Junction and thoroughly enjoyed it, and found ourselves not very far apart about what must be done. The question why a chap like that should completely alter his attitude when representing his members and how to stop him doing so is probably the most

5
LEFT LUGGAGE
SUBWAY
REFRESHMENTS

important single national question to-day.

And so in stages to Reading where I joined a diesel multiple-unit to Paddington. There were seven in our section. Six quiet people and one woman dressed as for the Grand Circle at Covent Garden and full of eloquence and emotion. Pity it was about railways and the iniquities of this DMU in particular. 'We used' she cried to an obviously bored husband 'to have respectable coaches and engines from Newbury. Now we have these rattle traps. We can't even stagger to the loo. We can't read or write or sleep or even talk unless we shout.' Husband looked as if he wished even more that her vocal chords would give out under the strain. Eventually – and I know better now – I said: 'Excuse me, Madam. I am a manager on this railway. May I ask you to look round. Out of seven people in this section three are reading, one is apparently asleep and one, myself, is writing.' She went through the roof in one athletic bound. Ealing is nine minutes from Paddington. A very long time.

LOST PROPERTY: I

Losing things has always bothered me; my own, naturally; my wife's, naturally – until I found out that the cry: 'I've lost my handbag' meant only that she had put it in a pretty natural, safe place, turned round three times and lost her way back to it; so that my 'How much was in it?!!' gave way over the years to a methodical recollection of where I had seen her go in the last minutes and the 'Here you are, darling.' Even more than hers and mine, losing things on the railway bothered me most. Railwaymen are by definition homo sapiens erectus. Mankind is, among his other faults, careless, casual, slipshod and often light-fingered. By the nature of man we *should* lose things on the railway. But a railway manager

Birmingham Snow Hill station was closed when services on the former GWR route through the city were switched to LMS New Street station as part of the rationalisation that accompanied electrification of the route from Euston in 1967. Now there are plans to bring local services back to Snow Hill as part of rail revitalisation in the West Midlands.

has to select, train and supervise homo sapiens, erectus railwayanus to rise above his nature at work so that the service is safe, punctual and reliable. That was my job.

That I was not doing it came to me most vividly when I dined in a regimental cavalry mess. My speech, made when flown with insolence and wine, had been about how wonderful our railway was, particularly Paddington and points west. It had seemed to go all right until a galloping major had got up and said: 'The other day we sent a train load of Bren Carriers to Salisbury Plain. They have got lost. Why? How?' Good questions, which perplexed me no end. A whole train . . . vividly identifiable as military . . . headed at the start in the right direction . . . enginemen and guard . . . yard inspectors . . . control. All along the line some railwaymen knew where it was going . . . or did they? So the inspiration, however discreditable, for the answer descended on me. I said: 'Did you put a label on it?' Incredibly a slow expression of doubt spread over his face, followed by complete mental paralysis. The mess laughed till the gunpowder ran out of the heels of their boots.

Nevertheless, next day when we still could not find this train and were saving our faces with the thought that it might have done a Philby behind the Curtain, my heart was down with the gunpowder in my boots. Now, Paddington was always kind to foreigners. They didn't take to the attitudes so if the Old Man's heart was in his boots they rallied to his side. On this day they said: 'Go and see the other side of it. It's the first day of the Lost Property Sale.'

A good idea. I rang Mr Duke and betook myself across the station to the second floor of the warehouse. Digressing – a little while before, flown with insolence and Beeching, I had said to the Goods Agent at Taunton who was not doing too well with his storage on the ground floor, 'What would happen if we took your storage away?' He reflected for a minute – wondering, as I realised later, what sort of a general manager I was – and then said: 'The top floors would fall in.' Welsh of course. Never miss a chance.

'Tuesday, 20 July, 1965. Sale of Miscellaneous Goods lying

in Warehouse at the Goods Warehouses, Paddington Station. Anstey, Horne and Co. . . . To sell by auction at 10.30am. Mr Duke took me up to the second floor. Low, dark, enormous. Ranged into the dim distance were the piles of Lots to be sold. In the centre rows of wooden benches. About fifty buyers, four fifths of them men. On the station side a small dais with a table and two chairs for the auctioneer and his clerk. Little formality. Tall, erect, dark hair and moustache with a small white pointed beard. And a cockney accent. 'I'm here in the bloody middle' he said once. Probably not either Mr Anstey or Mr Horne.

He started to sell at the rate of – I never can keep away from Time – 11 lots in 10 minutes. And my spirits started to rise. BR(WR) can lose a train load of Bren Carriers. Our lovely customers have left behind umbrellas: 3168 ladies, 887 gents; 980 scarves; 49 rings; 90 watches; bicycles; tricycles; radios; record players; cameras; a guitar; a violin; a mountain of clothing and much besides. I began to identify the buyers; regulars mostly said Mr Duke. Miller, Singer, Abel, Knight, Temore, Allaway, Dobeney, Cornish, Hutchings. They sat impassive in rows on the hard benches, muscles going rythmically in their jaws, eyes screwed up, flicking round the room, a lift of the catalogue, a twitch or occasionally a word for a bid. 'Why not' cried the auctioneer before long, 'start with a reasonable bid?'

'Why not' thought I, 'finish with a reasonable bid?' A zoom ciné camera for £9; 24 cameras in a suitcase for £2; 100 scarves for £6; Mr Cornish had 24 lined raincoats for £6.10s. An unidentified woman 30 women's coats for £3, as the women came in to bid when the umbrellas, the camping equipment, the hockey sticks, the rings, the watches, the cameras and the electric shavers were gone.

The auctioneer was getting hoarse. He called for a tea break and sucked peppermints. I began to reflect on what and how people leave behind. I remembered finding Elliott in the Lost Property Office at Kings Cross on his birthday sitting in a sailing dinghy with two of his staff singing shanties. I told this to Duke and found myself before long with the catalogue for the first-ever sale on my knee. 'Happy reading' said Mr Duke.

'Paddington. Clearance Sale of the Great Western Railway Company . . . Unclaimed Property. . . . Which will be sold by Auction by Messrs. Eversfield and Horne At the Great Western Auction Mart, Paddington Green on Thursday, June 21st 1855 at 10 for 11.' Like inviting people for a dinner. Hand in hand with a stately age. And so back through the years to Charles Stuart Calverley 'Thoughts on a Railway Station':

> 'Tis but a box of modest deal
> Directed to no matter where
> Yet down my cheeks the teardrops steal.
> Yes, I am blubbering like a seal.
> For on it is this mute appeal,
>   "With Care."
>
> 'Hast thou ne'er seen rough pointsmen spy
> Some simple English phrase "With Care"
> Or "This side uppermost" and cry
> Like children? No? No more have I.
> Yet deem not him whose eyes are dry
>   A tear.
>
> 'But ah! what treasure lies beneath
> That lid so much the worse for wear.
> A ring perhaps. A rosy wreath.
> A photograph by Vernon Heath.
> Some matron's temporary teeth
>   Or hair.'

Neat, economical English. A beautiful turn of phrase. Close observation. For in the 1855 catalogue all the items which may be under the lid appear except the temporary teeth – and those I found myself a century later. But that is another, and the next, story.

In 1855 our customers' habits were much the same about umbrellas, scarves, clothing, rings, and watches. They dressed up more. 'Lady's rich mantle'; 'Scarlet jacket and loops.' 'Freemason's apron, swordbelt and patterns of mosaic charm' bought by Robertson for 4/–. Much to do with a horse; in breeches, saddles, horse cloths and currycombs. It was a hunting man who left behind 'a saddle, five bridles, headstall, muzzle, strap and chain, girth and four horse shoes'! And an umpire who travelled with 'three cricket bats, six stumps, a portable seat and a cane' although a question hangs over this identification.' The bats and the seat are at odds. Someone required 'Porcupine quilles, 12 razors and cases, eight pocket knives, corkscrew, piece of horn, four scent bottles, two portmonnaies, tobacco box and gutta percha tube'. An author, well-to-do, prolific and a bit of a fop, Watson.

But who will enlighten me about lot 105? (Evans, £1); 'Portmanteau and contents comprising curling tongs, two pair boots, two pair shoes, trouser's straps, three pair gloves, two powder flasks, razor strop, six books, set of shoe brushes, two hair brushes and combs, two bags, palettes, shaving brush, cigar case, pewter bottle, three tin boxes, two balls, two razors in case, sponge, nipple wrench, gum brush, two lasts, measuring tape, pair of cuffs, tooth brush and paper knife.' Here we have, who? Literate, but not an author. Painter maybe. Careful of his appearance. Powder flasks and two balls suggest a duellist. The cause? Well, Charlie Chaplin in *Modern Times* on a production line frantically turning two nuts every second as they surge past and in his lunch hour, still twitching, out on the street tightening the nuts on the front of the women's jackets – nipple-wrench? But why not a do-it-himself job?

I came back from these agreeable fancies reluctantly; from Eversfield and Horne to Anstey and Horne. The room was now thinning fast. The auctioneer had been replaced by another with a black moustache which drooped forlornly over his jowls. He was leaning in my direction and his clerk was shaking his head. Duke had not kept proper control of me. In my abstraction the 1855 catalogue had waved and I had bought 1965, lot 550, an airgun with target. And I would not have wanted the target. I had several in mind at Marylebone Headquarters. But they rescued me by introducing Mr Allaway at 55/–. So Marylebone Man went on unscathed, sitting down to meals. At that they were lucky. In 1855 I could not have bought an airgun. It would have been Lot 23, 'one crossbow'.

My morale was now high. Losing an occasional train of Bren Carriers was pardonable, almost praiseworthy when these throwaways were the fathers and mothers of railwaymen. When I got home I said to Jean: 'Do you ever take off your wedding ring?' She tried and couldn't. So that question answered itself, but left open the six lost wedding rings in the sale. Was there a lost wife with each? But that too is another story.

LOST PROPERTY: II

'He was going too fast' said the Chief Civil Engineer – comfortably as one who knows that this time he is beyond paradventure in the right.

'What do you mean by too fast?' I asked.

'More than the 75 permitted, anyway, You said yourself, Sir? – Barney called me 'Sir' only when more than usually self-righteous – 'that you clocked him at 88 just afterwards.'

'I know' I said. 'Nevertheless, we ought to be able to go through Twyford on the Main Line at 88 without the upper jaw of a set of false teeth leaping from the lower and cartwheeling in the aisle.'

Slowly, very slowly, the self-righteous look faded from Barney's face. For a full half-minute he fixed his eye on mine, peering for the red glint of lunacy, which would send him scapering to pass the buck to Doctor Claude Newnham.

'F-false teeth?'

'They were on the table in front of me. I had just sat down for lunch. Listen.'

Sitting as I was in the chair which had supported the august bottoms of Felix Pole, James Milne and Keith Grand, I had the advantage of him. He could not choose but hear.

'Listen', I said, 'and it will distract you for twenty minutes from thinking about Arthur Butland at the BRB and the iniquities of your budget.

'Yesterday I went in the general direction of Worcester on the 11.45. I went straight in for lunch, lifted my napkin and found a set of false teeth. Upper and lower they were, set precisely one on the other so that the bite was right. They were facing me. They were not only grinning but grinning at *me*.

'I looked at them, sort of hoping for an answer but there they were, clenched and uncommunicative. And I was sure in that moment, just as I am sure that the dog's hindleg in the Down Main Line at Twyford is one too, that a great Managerial Hogsnorton was under way.'

Barney said: 'The speed order at Twyford . . .' but I interrupted. 'We haven't got there yet. Where we have got to is to where Charles the Steward came in and saw'.

'Sir!' he cried.

'Not mine' I said, and bared my own at him. 'Whose then?'

Charles didn't know. So we began to consider the problem. 'We laid this cover not half-an-hour ago' said Charles. 'They weren't there then. They belong to someone on the train.'

'Are they someone's spare set?' but a shred of bacon proved that they were in current use.

'So there's a gentleman on the train without his teeth.'

'Fair enough, Charles. These are no female nibblers. Look at the eye-teeth, I tell you; all the better to bite you with.'

Charles advanced the theory that someone wished to reserve his place for lunch. I dismissed this.

'Why, if so, hide them under the napkin? They would have been in the open, defying all comers.'

We considered suicide – no, in principle you commit suicide ship-shape and Bristol fashion with your teeth in place so that whoever finds you thinks what a loss you are to society. We reflected on a punch-up; teeth out, gumshield in and wham! And this theory lay on the table, as we took, Barney, your ridiculous speed order at Twyford at admittedly more than the speed which you allow.'

Barney made no attempt to intervene. He also looked clenched and uncommunicative.

The upshot was that the upper jaw leapt off the lower, bounced once on the table and galloped along the floor, to the feet of the Travelling Ticket Collector who had just come through the swing door.

'I will say this, Barney, the Western trains its staff to a hair in public relations. Not a muscle moved in the face of this iron man. He picked up the teeth, whipped a napkin off the nearest table, dusted them, placed them in the exact centre of the napkin and handed them to me with the respect due to the heir of Sir Felix Pole, Sir James Milne and Keith Grand.

'Not mine' I said again.

'We now had three in committee but no more light. So I proceeded to Instant Management.

'We have two choices' I said. 'Either you, Charles, take these teeth round the train on a salver when you call the first lunch and call the teeth at the same time; or you, Snapper, when you examine tickets examine also the mouths of examinees, not bothering of course with the females.

'One of these days I shall learn, Barney, some of the things that the Woking Staff College and the print-outs from our splendid computer don't seem to include. One of them is that an Instant Manager should never give the staff a choice. Like Denis Compton calling for a run, it is an invitation to debate.'

Charles and Snapper promptly recollected that the duty of the staff when consulted is to offer suggestions to improve the ideas of management. Snapper it was who produced the punch-line.

'Seems to me' he said, 'that these 'ere are Lost Property. That's the Guard's job.'

And here we were in a demarcation dispute. And, not only that, but the managerial hogsnorton was now well developed. Reluctantly I, Muggins, wrapped the teeth in a napkin, hoped as a parting shot at Charles that I wouldn't come back to find in the place, lately and jointly occupied by the teeth and myself, some VIP, speechless with rage and inarticulation, mumbling Charles' steak with toothless gums. I set off for the brake van.

'When I got there I saw at a glance that my journey had been unnecessary. This guard was one of those towering, resplendent figures who, in the days of the Great Western, clad in finest broadcloth, topped off with a kind of fez surmounted by a pom-pom, conducted only Peers of the

Realm and Lords Lieutenant to their accustomed seats and earned the Company its equally towering reputation for public service.'

At this Barney stirred. He felt the rush of life along his keel. At Paddington no man can denigrate the Company any more than he can speak sharply about Brunel. And however deep was Barney's coma while he was awaiting his chance to get the agenda more relevant to Railway Civil Engineering, these terms of praise for the Company still penetrated.

He said: 'When Brunel built this railway he made it the best in the world; and a lot of people kept it so for more than a hundred years' – meaning, till some 'erbs like you got hold of it. Stuffy, I thought.

So I said: 'Did Brunel build Twyford like a dog's hind leg? Reflect on this while I finish my tale. So I asked this guard, purely as an academic question, what he would do if he found or had handed to him some Lost Property. He would, so he said, look after it until he returned to Paddington. He would then Deliver it to the Porter in Attendance, (he tended to talk in Capitals) for Transmission to the Lost Property Office.

'Once again, therefore, this last of my staff in this train proved a broken reed. I emerged into the corridor carrying what was now obviously My Napkin and My False Teeth and My Management Problem; or the Can, if you like.

'From the first lavatory a long thin grey figure, drooping on his stem, emerged and tried to walk through me. 'I'm ffo forry' he mumbled. "I've loft my ffpectaclef. I can't see an inff wiffout ffem." '

'Your spectacles, Sir' I said, 'are on your nose. But here are your teeth.'

Upper and lower snapped into place.

'Thank you so much, Sir' he said. 'I can't see to eat without them.'

Barney was now bolt upright.

'Out of all the questions to ask . . .' he began.

'Start with why Brunel built Twyford like a dog's hindleg' I interrupted. 'A narrow bridge at one end and a wide platform immediately beyond.'

This threw him off course.

'Brunel never . . .' he began again.

'OK Barney. Let's get back to Brunel.'

And do you know, we did. He chopped a large chunk out of the platform, realigned the down main and raised the limit to 90. Maybe by now he is equipping the line for the atmospheric railway. Broad Gauge, of course.

LOST PROPERTY: III

When I get in a sleeper I go straight to bed. The sleeping car attendant arriving five minutes later to say: 'Gold Pass 112 and tea at 6.30 as usual?' finds me down to my pants. This is Management Policy – to get to sleep before we start and not to try to manage. Otherwise any unusual operating or mechanical or civil engineering noise keeps me wide awake and wondering whether I should pay official attention to it. I know that if I do pay such attention, I shall almost always be getting in the way; and secondly that there are people on the train already, capable of dealing with any emergency. On the other hand, I enjoy emergencies.

In conformity with this policy I was asleep and fearing no evil when the attendant opened the door, touched my shoulder, put on the light and ushered in a female. For this the LNER had not prepared me in my training. Mother taught me always to stand up in the presence of a lady. I had never asked her: 'In pyjamas, with the cord probably loose?' because the answer would have been short and sharp about wearing pyjamas in mixed company. I compromised by getting up on one elbow and blinking at her. Her cord was not loose. She wasn't wearing one. A short nightdress, a little overlay. An invitation to Instant Love.

She said in a flat, precise voice: 'I've lost my husband.'

I looked at the sleeping car attendant. Albert is his name. Albert shrank himself to his full width. His eyes glazed. His cheeks distended. His head sunk into his shoulders. He assumed the general demeanour and, as far as he could, the appearance of a stuffed frog. This is one of the standard ploys of a railwayman in face of an unusual and probably disagreeable duty. He does not refuse it. He does not run away from it. He does not blow his whistle and take his train rapidly away. He just makes himself invisible.

'Albert' I said, tentatively. 'This lady has lost her husband.' And what with the sure and certain conviction that a nonsense was developing and what with Albert's mantle of invisibility, my cheeks too were distended with dealing with and suppressing tears of laughter and joy.

Albert remained in status, so to speak, quo. So I took the first step, forward and downward.

'Where?' I said with a faint echo of some picture or other, 'did you last see your husband?'

'In bed' she said without enthusiasm.

'In whose bed?'

This was me talking. You have to remember that I had just been woken from a lovely sleep and that I was in the dream-like presence of a stuffed frog whose name was Albert and believed himself to be invisible. But I know I should not have said it. She slapped my face with her first sudden show of enthusiasm. And I was glad that Albert, being a frog, saw no evil, heard no evil and would speak no evil of me up and down the railway.

Both of us, the exception being Albert, were now wide awake. I got the story. She and her husband had joined the train at Kings Cross. They had gone to bed in adjacent first-class sleepers with the communicating door open. She had lain awake listening to the general rush and clatter of the train, which Henry Longhurst says you can subdue by putting the plug in the wash basin and shutting the lid. After a long time she had switched on the dim light and had seen that no head lay on the pillow next door.

She had searched for him, she said, 'high and low'. Not, come to that, there is much 'low' in a BR sleeper. You can look, if you like, under the bed; but it would be a real shaver of a husband whom you would find there. Digressing, I always chuckle when I think back to the issue of the *600 Magazine* which had an illustration of a bedroom, with a single bed, rumpled, by whose side lay a pair of bedroom slippers and a nightdress. The caption was 'I always wondered what I would do if I found a Man under my bed.' If you can't beat 'em, join 'em. Anyway she did not find him high in the rack or low under the bed. It was odd that she expected to but then the whole sequence was odd. I thought nothing of it and I am sure Albert didn't either.

So, after a while, having abandoned hope that he was in the loo and would come back she came to look for the Proper Authorities (all in Capitals) and found Albert who found me before doing his 'Heigh-ho says Rowley' withdrawal into another dimension.

Contemplating Albert, now deep in hibernation and protective colouring, I could see his point. The Great British Public whom we serve take intrusions into their sleeping quarters in no cordial spirit. Their reaction, male or female, to the question 'Have you got this lady's husband here?' is liable to be sharp. A disagreeable duty for Albert. And of course he could avoid it if rematerialised, by saying either 'This lady's husband is a Missing Person i'n't he? That's a job for the Police' or 'He's her property, i'n't he? And she's lost him. Lost Property's the Guard's job.'

The train rushed on noisily and smoothly through the night. After a little I tightened my pyjama cord and put the plug in the wash basin to see whether Henry Longhurst assisted thought. He didn't. However, chivalry prevailed. I made up my mind that I was not going into anyone's sleeper, but I would draw the rest of the train for this character. There was plenty of it. As well as sleepers two or three ordinary coaches, several vans of mails and parcels and of course the Night Cap Bar.

By this time I had a pullover and a macintosh over my pyjamas. Albert was still standing in the door way. It is one of the penalties of dematerialisation that you must not move or even flicker; otherwise the chap looking at you stops believing that you are not there. The Roman sentry at Pompeii, who was immolated in ash from Vesuvius had probably got himself into that frame of mind. So had the splendid fireman clad in full oilskins and helmet, standing rigid guard over a wrecked coach at an accident at Welwyn. After an hour I found he was obscuring a human leg, protruding from the rear of the coach. 'No, he hadn't seen it. How could he have? He hadn't got eyes in the back of his head, had he?'

In order to make room and, I suppose, to keep warm the wife had now tucked herself up cosily in my bed. So, being as ready as I ever should be I asked her how I should identify her husband. She gave me a picture of a sort of Uncle of Tarzan, seven feet high, five feet wide, bulging with muscle and beetling with eyebrows. 'He is limping a little and has a strip of plaster on his left cheek.' Maybe she kicked him and hit him with a frying pan with the same athletic movement.

I went into the corridor walking through Albert. This made him hit his head on the door and brought him again among us. 'Albert' I said, 'Before I go down the train let us look at the passenger list. Not, you understand, with any evil thoughts whatever. But the great and good Doctor told me to evaluate all possible solutions.'

Albert said cryptically: 'It's chucking out day from Parliament'.

'Albert!' I said. 'Be yourself . . . how many?'

'Two peers' said Albert, 'One peeress; seven MP's, two of them female.'

I looked at the list. 'We're all right Albert' I said. 'I know that Madame du Barry was asked at the age of seventy when passion left a woman and she replied 'My dear, you must ask someone far older than me'. But she was French. He will be in the Night Cap Bar.'

And I set off down the train. The first two lavatories showed themselves 'vacant' and were. The third shewed 'vacant' and contained a bloke in a position in which he was not limping. He wore no plaster. I went quickly on and came to the Night Cap Bar. Sam was still there. A career of tending bars, rushing up and down the railway line by night, inducing an alcoholic stupor in sleeping cars has given Sam a long and drooping form, an eerie pallor, a gift for quotation and many illusions, most of which come true.

I put the problem.

'There was a whole bunch in here' he said. 'This Tarzan with them. They don't like their bed same as you, not unless there's an Objective, if you take my meaning.'

I had once told Sam about Management by Objective. Indeed he had a target of Royal Scot miniatures and much else by which he was judged. It was good that at least he had remembered the jargon, even if he had translated and corrupted the High Ideal.

'He'll be with . . .' said Sam.

'Sam!' I said.

'Age' he said gloomily, 'will not weary *them*.'

I betook myself back through the swaying corridors, minded to tell this wife that he was in the Night Cap Bar and would be home with the milk; thereby prolonging a marriage and getting my bed back.

As I opened my door I was conscious of a presence in the corridor, Tarzan in person. He said: 'I've lost my wife'. Then he saw. 'Laura!' he cried.

If you have ever dug for lançons in the estuaries in Brittany you will know how when your spade scoops one up, with a flash and a wriggle it is out of sight yards away in the wet sand. So Laura leapt from bed, eeled under his arm and was gone.

Tarzan bent a look on me. The eyebrows twitched together. He leaned toward me, champing his jaw muscles. Then he turned on his heel and padded away.

In the morning I made it my business to get up very slowly; but when I emerged from the train he was waiting at the barrier. I faced a fate worse than death with the aplomb given to those who have had a lifetime of railway management and of the Great British Public.

He padded up to me. He took my arm but instead of shaking it like a gorilla he massaged it and said:

'Thanks a million, old chap.'

WESTERN

To: H. M. Lattimer, Esq.,   *From*: General Manager
H. C. Sanderson, Esq.,   Paddington.

Shall we pull these guys' legs? What about the attached as a quiz in the next Management Bulletin?
Improve and amplify.

Punctuality of express trains

1. Would you time a train:—
   a. Up to the speed which the locomotive horse power allows having regard to P.S.Rs.
   b. With a calculated allowance for T.S.R.s
   c. With (b) plus an allowance for not-so-good engine driver not-well-signalmen taking chances with freight trains.
2. Would you request a special stop for:–

   The Queen
   The Prime Minister
   A Divisional Manager
   A passenger who has misread the timetable
   Your Aunt Fanny
   Yourself
3. Would you delay a train for:–
   Passengers queueing at the booking office
   Passengers running down the hill to the station
4. Would you blow a whistle at:–
   Passengers saying tender farewells to their sweetie-pies
             strolling up trains to their usual compartments
   The Beatles
5. Would you say anything, and if so, what, to a guard who delayed a train by:–
   Leaving platform staff to do the work receiving and signing for Union funds from a branch official
6. Would you strengthen a train beyond the engine load to:–
   Avoid overcrowding?

Convey the General Manager's saloon?
Get empty stock out of your hair?
7. Would you load in a train:–
Parcels or Mails beyond the capacity of the receiving
station to unload in the booked time?
The chassis of a Rover car?
Traffic in front of rear brakes which would require drawing
up at the receiving station?
Parcels traffic at your own station if it required drawing
up?
Any marks less than 100% disqualifies from being an Area
Manager, or any other Manager.

MEMORANDUM

To: Divisional Manager,   *From*: G. Fiennes
CARDIFF.   19.1.65

I have just been reading your tireless self in the
Commercial and Industrial Review. Good stuff.

Being one of the small minority which uses abuse and
sarcasm (and so leaves you unmoved) will you say
whether we had better try unfailing kindness as a
management technique.

6

British Railways within the centre – and without

PUBLIC RELATIONS

In the 1950s British Railways decided that public relations were A GOOD THING. This was curious as we were under military government at the time, with Generals Sir Brian Robertson, Llewellyn Wansborough Jones, Daryl Watson and Field Marshal Slim. One or two of them had been very close to Monty. And the first thing they did was to say 'the British Railways image is *shocking*.' Something must be done. And the second thing was to produce a new crest, in which that emasculated lion rides rather uncomfortably on a wheel. The second change was to alter the colour of everything. This in future years became a habit so that all trains are still going about piebald. And they instituted a series of experiments, trying it on the public, as to the sort of colour that the public would prefer. It was rather odd seeing what austere people they were that they were dedicated in this choice of colour almost entirely to fattening foods. We had plum and spilt milk, we had strawberries and cream, and we had chocolate and cream. And the third thing they did was to tell all their Managers that when there was thunder and lightning from Southern commuters to stop hiding under the bed, but to go out and face the music. And fourthly they gave us Public Relations Officers. Mine was a retired Naval Commander who certainly never hid under a bed in his life. But as he'd been a member of the silent service, on the Great Northern Line it was clearly a do-it-myself job. And this was new. Until then I had had 30 years on the railway, trying to make the railways safe, frequent, fast, punctual, comfortable and

149

economic. But never in the shop front. I was one of 'THEY'. Faceless, indifferent, dim-witted, malignant. All of which I was more recently called in the press about closing branch lines, particularly by a church organist whom I eventually put completely to rout by pointing out that the church was withdrawing services just as fast as British Railways. And as a public relations exercise this was not particularly clever, because it didn't endear me to him.

I had to go out then and do it myself. I never discovered what the rules were. It was trial and error and a great deal more error than trial.

Probably the way not to do it is summed up by the announcement that we heard in Manchester a year or two earlier which said smoothly, 'We apologise for the train which has just arrived at number five platform. This was due to delay.'

But if there was a rule I suppose the first one is Tell the Truth. And I thought this would be a good plan. So we issued instructions to our stations that they must put over sensible announcements apologising for trains being late, and that when trains were late guards must go up and down the train and tell the people why.

There was not a very good public reaction to this, because the stories about engine failure and wagons being derailed further up the line and technical hitches became very quickly a bit stale. So one day I took myself to King's Cross and into the broadcaster's room and said 'Have you got anything about that's late?' And she said, 'Oh, yes, the Yorkshire Pullman is just past Finsbury Park. He's 35 minutes late.' I told her what I wanted her to say. She said, 'Sir, I can't put that over.' I said, 'Yes, you can, of course you can. I'm telling you to. I'm the line manager.' She said, 'It's as much as my job is worth.' So I said, 'Well, you clear out of the seat and I'll say it.' The Yorkshire Pullman ran in and I gave it a minute for the people to alight on the platform and I then said smoothly into the loudspeaker. 'British Transport Commission very much regret the delay to the Yorkshire Pullman which has just arrived at Platform 5. This was due to bad management.' I then raced down to see the effect. Either the thing had not been heard, which I doubt because some of the staff had heard it, or the people were completely disinterested in bad management, because there was not a ripple on the surface.

However, I wasn't discouraged by this. I thought that I should pursue matters. And about three weeks later I was riding on a train from Doncaster to King's Cross, and we came to a stand at Hitchin; the engine had had a hot axlebox. So we were clearly going to be more than the ten minutes late which was on the instructions. I went to find the guard and I looked in the rear brake and he wasn't there. So I went along to the middle of the train and there he was. I said, 'We're late'. 'Yes' 'Are you going to tell the train why?' 'No', he wasn't. 'Well have you seen the instructions from the Line Traffic Manager that when trains are more than 10 minutes late the guard should go along the train and tell the people why?' 'Yes, he'd seen that, but the Line Traffic Manager wasn't his boss, Mr Huskisson was his boss.' 'Well, I'm the Line Traffic Manager and where do we go from there?' We looked at each other and then we started on the proper democratic process of negotiation; the upshot, after some minutes, was a proper democratic conclusion that he would go and tell the front half of the train and I would go and tell the rear half. So I set off, opening compartment doors, 'The British Transport Commission regrets to announce . . .' and so on. And I got quite a number of nods, I got one smile, two or three people snarled, when I got to the last compartment this was full of enginemen, drivers and firemen, riding home on the cushions. I hesitated outside there for a minute, wondering whether to or whether not. And eventually came to the conclusion that I should have a go. And I opened the compartment door and said 'Gentlemen, the British Transport Commission regret to announce that the engine has had a hot axlebox. It is being changed and we shall be 28 minutes late at King's Cross.' There was a deathly hush. I stood there with the calm resolution on my face, I hope, of a public servant carrying out an unpleasant duty with resolution. They, on their side, you could see the wheels going round in their heads. Who is this guy? Is he a railwayman? If he is a railwayman, is he something in authority?' If those three things, is he taking the mickey out of us, which I suppose I was. Finally the senior driver dealt with the situation. He looked up with a froglike expression on his face, and said 'Guv'nor, what is a hot axlebox?'

I remember somebody in Oxford spending a first-class fare from Oxford to Paddington and back, in order to storm into my office, and tell me what had happened to him that morning. He'd gone to the booking office, and he said, 'Day return Banbury, please' and the booking clerk had said '8s 3d' And the chap said, 'Well, look, I booked one from Banbury to Oxford only ten days ago, and they charged me 7s 9d' The booking clerk looked owlishly through the window at him and said, 'But it's up hill'. Now in fact this was just as good an answer as anything else. You play the market in accordance with what you can get from the market, and if from a large town, Oxford, you can get 8s 3d to Banbury, and from a smaller town, Banbury, you can only get 7s 9d to Oxford, this is precisely what a railway should do. Nevertheless, as a matter of Public Relations, you mustn't jape with people west of Liverpool Street.

From these rather hesitating, probably disastrous, beginnings, we gradually got better, and of course the real thing about public relations is to make them all unnecessary by running the perfect service, and having everybody believing you. If you can't do that, and I don't know any railway in the world that does, then the next best thing is to distract attention by some form of gimmick. In the West Country we were always suspected of malignantly running down the railway in order to close it.

When I got back to the Eastern Region, I found that they'd gone all serious and they were actually teaching public relations to people at our Ilford School. They were having classes for ticket collectors, and platform foremen, and porters in how to behave to the public. As a new General Manager, of course, I went down to have a look at this new activity; rather spoilt the proceedings by saying that what I really thought was wanted was to teach the British Public not to be beastly to British Railways, rather than to teach railwaymen how not to be beastly to the British Public, but that naturally had no effect at all and the proceedings went on as before. And the sort of tour de force of the whole proceedings was the horror film, which was to demonstrate visually to this audience what a terrible thing it was not to treat the public properly. There was one of our new booking offices, large plate glass windows, and inside those plate glass windows, there were two girls as the booking clerks nattering with their backs to the window. A customer comes up to the window, one of the girls looks over her shoulder and sees that he is there, and goes on with her nattering, and the chap stands there. After a minute he looks at this watch; stands some more; takes his hat off, and he scratches his head; puts his hat back on his head and looks at his watch. This goes on

Forward planning or changing circumstances? Carlisle marshalling yard nearing completion in the early 1960s. With the abandonment of wagon-load in favour of train-load traffics following Beeching principles in the later 1960s and the development of Merry-go-Round trains the need for such yards was virtually eliminated and Carlisle yard became an expensive white elephant. (*London Midland Region, BR*)

for about a minute, and then the film is switched off and one of the instructors says very smoothly, 'And now class, please tell me, what was wrong with this sequence?' A hot and angry voice from the back, 'Bloke did nofffinck to help his bleeding self, did he?' The crashing cockney logic which always goes completely to the root of the matter. And although we certainly went on teaching public relations, I don't think we talked to them quite like that.

MERRY-GO-ROUND

'Merry-go-Round' said Glyn England, the then Chairman of the Central Electricity Generating Board, 'is the greatest single advance in freight transport since the coming of the railways.' This was in a lecture to the Institute of Mechanical Engineers. And in a memoir of this kind it should have its place. And if it is a brag, then it is a brag because alone I did it – well – not the nuts and bolts but the idea.

I had been down to High Marnham Power Station on the Friday and stood in unbelief while a train of wagons was tippled one by one into hoppers and then one which had wet coal was 'vibrated'. That set my teeth on edge. On Sunday I had a bath. We have very different policies about baths. Jean fills her to her plimsol line, scuffles around and is out in four minutes. I fill mine to the neck, slightly hotter than is comfortable, lie back and let my thoughts mingle with steam. I forget if I even wash. On this occasion my thoughts were not all that pleasant, that vibrator shaking the wagon to bits always prevailing. Slowly the dream changed and I saw forty tons of coal sliding smoothly through a bottom door into the hopper – *and the train was still moving.* Why not? A loop railway. Hoppers at the power station, an overhead bunker at the colliery. Round and round – the train without stopping. Merry-go-Round. Power station coal; steel works; aggregates – there was no end to it. And in fact the last I heard seventy-million tons were being carried by Merry-go-Round and if it had not been for the miners' strike the total would be heading for a hundred million.

The beginning of the new order on BR in the 1960s with block coal trains, this one seen on the Midland main line alongside the M1 motorway at Mill Hill. At this stage not much else had changed but the Merry-go-Round principle of loading and unloading specially designed hopper wagons on the move at collieries and power stations was being developed. (*London Midland Region, BR*)

In the morning I wrote a half page to Frank Gray, the head of our Costing Service. He said: 'This will reduce the cost of bulk transport by at least three-quarters.' So a note to Glyn England, the Engineer of the CEGB and to Derek Ezra of the Coal Board. We met. Glyn England saw the point at once. He stopped the design of all power stations of which there were several until he had had a look at the method. Derek was in some difficulty. As a start my Lord Robens then Chairman of the Coal Board and my Lord Beeching had gone into the rutting season. All these herds of empty wagons standing about at collieries. 'You shall pay for the time these stand empty' bellowed Beeching. 'We never have' roared Robens 'and aren't going to start now.' Well – that was one. The other was that the NCB's capital expenditure was fully committed. However, Derek saw our point and promised good will.

Then came a stroke of luck. Scotland was designing a new power station at Cockenzie just south of Edinburgh and a new colliery, Monkton Hall, to serve it. All was in the early stages of design. They submitted plans shewing arrival sidings, departure lines, engine spurs, tipplers, vibrators and all and a request for 550 wagons. We wrote back and said: 'If you do it like this (with a minimal sketch) you will want none of these things and only 44 wagons. There was an exceedingly short delay and the answer came back, with sketches, and a request for 44 wagons.

The Mechanical Engineers did a quick and good job on vernier control on locomotives to give us a speed through the unloading shed of between one and a quarter miles an hour. We debated at length between 100 ton bogie wagons and four wheelers but English coal is sticky and the valley angle has to be 60% so the four wheeler won the day. Somehow, no snags, no delays. So there is Merry-go-Round. My only regret is that the first scheme was in Scotland where of course the writ of two of the three originators Glyn England, and Derek Ezra did not run. Nevertheless it was I who had the bath and the golden dream.

MY PART IN THE GREAT TRAIN ROBBERY

It is always fun – or nearly always – when Institutions and the Establishment (all in Capital Letters written in by the people who institute and establish) fall into derision. And, if someone had not knocked the enginemen of the Up Postal about – quite badly – the whole of the Great Train Robbery would have been good clean fun. Even as it was, my part in it was fun. I was then Chief Operating Officer of British Railways at 222 Marylebone Road. As Marylebone Man I was both an Institution and an undeniable figure in the Establishment. As Chief Operating Officer I fell into derision because the whole thing was my fault.

It began quietly enough. The telephone by my bed purred

me awake. 'Control' said the smooth voice. 'The Up Postal has been stopped near Leighton Buzzard and the contents of the strong box have gone.' The message was in due form. Mark the absence of any suggestion that anyone had done anything, let alone was responsible for the thing done. It was strictly in line with the normal 'so-and-so has become derailed'. The only suggestion of human agency was in the words 'been stopped'. The contents of the strong box *prima facie* had simply taken themselves off. Nevertheless, there was a suppressed sense of the thing being not run-of-the-mill which came through to me. The Chief Controller's voice held a preturnatural gravity which meant one, or both, of two things; either that the event was abnormally grave or that he expected me to say something which would give him a laugh. I got in first. I said 'Gone – *have* they?' and laughed.

I got up and set off for the Kremlin. The story as then known was a simple one. The Up Postal had been stopped by signals. A gang had come aboard, had cowed the staff into running the front part of the train forward to a convenient spot and had robbed the train. It was clearly a highlight in railway history; but at that moment, which was after Euston had cleared the line, it seemed a business for the police and the Post Office rather than BR and it seemed secondly, that the Chief Operating Officer might be in the game but rather like a touch-judge, running about and waving a flag at people who had committed offences. If anyone was tearing his hair, it should have been my friend Brigadier Kenneth Holmes, the Director of Postal Services, who owned and staffed travelling post offices. This sense of well-being like that after a dose of phosgene gas lasted a few hours.

When dawn came and in due time the rest of the Establishment had established itself, people tried to convince me first that it was no laughing matter and secondly that it was my fault. 'They got away with two-and-a-half-million pounds' they said *avec empressement*, not realising that the sum took the whole affair higher into the cloud cuckoo land of laughter; and off they went to meetings which discussed our own £80m deficit *avec le sangfroid habituel* until 12.45

when the prior claims of executive lunches would prevail.

Life became temporarily more serious when Dr Beeching sent for me. 'The Postmaster-General' he said, 'is making a statement in the House of Commons that the robbery is the fault of British Railways because the regular vehicle with the proper Strong Box was not in the train. If it had been, the gang would not have been able to force it. Secondly he wants to go down to Willesden this afternoon to look at things and to decide what to do for the future.' It was one of the many good things about the great and good Doctor that he would stop at that point, leave his officers to get on with it and turn to other things, occasionally *The Times* Crossword.

I rang up Kenneth Holmes. We agreed a time to meet at Willesden.

'The PMG will be there' he said. 'The Ideas branch are down there already. They'll be cooking up something pretty drastic. By the way' he went on, 'Can we have something immediately by way of warning? Can your Controls tell the police when a Postal is held up for any unknown reason?'

'Well, the signalman knows if a train is an unduly long time in a section. He can tell Control and Control can tell the police.'

'When can we start that?'

'Tonight – if you really mean it. We may get some false alarms.'

'Yes, never mind. From to-night then.'

'I'll send you a copy of the instructions.' And so we did. The police made no bother about it but within a few days a Postal stopped miles from anywhere in Goucestershire. The procedure went click-click-click. The police barred the roads and lined the hedges. The driver, having rectified the defect on his diesel, drove briskly away; ignoring the fanfare of police whistles.

Meantime I went down to Willesden. Top security. The PMG was inspecting the regular vehicle with the strong, Strong Box. His henchmen barred my entry. When Kenneth had removed the obstruction I found the PMG looking gloomily at the strong, Strong Box. My spirits rose. It was obvious to me, and I suppose to him, that a resolute Boy Scout could have forced an entry with one of those things for taking stones out of horses' hooves. Neither of us communicated our thoughts to the other. He had already made his views public; and for me Manners Makyth Man. He had nevertheless taken the point because soon the GPO built a new range of travelling post offices and designed them to thwart Boy Scouts.

We went outside and were conducted in due form to where the Ideas Branch had prepared a whole range of devices. The first was a loud speaker which, when you tripped a button, set off an outcry designed to urge all good citizens to the rescue. 'THIS TRA-I-IN' it wailed, 'IS BEING ATTA-A-A-CKED BY BA-A-A-ANDITS'. I readily assented to this, having had recent experience of the readiness of the citizens to come to our aid. My wife, coming home from the church fete, spilled the takings on the way. 'Help' she cried as she always did in the face of an emergency. In a flash the path was full of willing helpers helping themselves. I mentioned this to Kenneth but he dismissed the idea, that the device might attract not good citizens but bad on a profit-sharing basis. In fact the only time on which the device worked was in the carriage sidings at York when someone – never identified – set it going. The mystery being top secret, no one in BR knew how to switch it off. So, until the clockwork or whatever ran down, the Banshee outcry rang over the City and over the Vale of York, summoning all good men. No one took any notice at all.

The second device – natural to a seafaring nation – was to summon aid by firing rockets. This was a first-ever. No one, except on Guy Fawkes' night, had ever fired a rocket from a train. A 15 inch naval gun, yes, but with the train all strapped down and with due regard to where the muzzle was pointing. And indeed would a rocket summon anyone but the crew of the life-boat?

I said at large: 'With all respect' (which means 'with no respect whatever') 'we should want some safeguards.'

'Such as?'

'Well, not firing under Euston or Rugby station roof; not

under a footbridge when a girl is walking across; not under the overhead wire which runs all the way to Manchester . . .'

'Ah' said they; 'we thought of that so we have staggered the spout to one side.'

'So' said I, 'does the wire stagger from side to side.'

'With all respect' they said; 'we thought of that too. So we have an alternative mounting underneath the coach which we are ready to demonstrate.'

We clambered down on to the permanent way. We retired to a very with-all-respectful distance indeed and, as far as we could judge, out of the line of fire.

'There will be' said the Ideas Branch, 'no rocket; only an explosion.'

I made no objection, however self-defeating was the idea of having no rocket; and how interesting the outcome would be of the alternative, firing a rocket sideways. I was hugging myself in the sure and certain promise that a Hogsnorton of spectacular proportions had hove over the horizon.

With due solemnity and with all deliberate speed they lit the fuse. The little trail of blue smoke snaked toward the coach, crept upwards and disappeared. There was a shattering explosion. We went forward through the smoke, treading in the remains of the coach's electric batteries. We peered at the wreck of the vacuum cylinders and distorted brake gear. We straightened up and saw that the driver of a pilot on the next siding but one was going about his lawful occasions, not taking the least notice of our crashing demand that he should stop what he was doing and come running.

'With all respect,' I said . . .

A GREAT NORTHERN JOURNEY

In 1965 the British Railways Board in agreement with the Government made up its mind to combine the Eastern and North Eastern regions. This was a logical decision. The two east coast regions had always been a virtual entity ever since the Great Northern 'Towns' route had been built and the stranglehold of King Hudson had been broken.

However, the decision to make York the headquarters and there to move some seven hundred people from London daunted the protagonists. And they searched high and low. Who should be the ram caught in the thicket. Eventually the lot fell on Matthias. I was summoned and offered the job with the grumpy words: 'You seem to be able to get people to work for you. I can't think why. So it had better be you.' Now I was supremely happy at Paddington. The best job on BRB. A closely knit team doing good work. A laugh a minute. I should have told him where he could put his job. But I suppose I have always been the girl who can't say 'No'. Anyway on 1 January 1966 I became for a year General Manager at Liverpool and General Manager designate, York.

Eastern Region General Manager Fiennes greets The Queen as she arrives from Kings Lynn at Liverpool Street on 6 February 1967. (*British Railways*)

The difficult part of the task was to persuade seven hundred wives to move. We used to take each week fifty or so down to York, give them a coach tour of the city, let them meet the Housing Manager and the House Agents, have tea and so home. Now one of the good things about being General Manager at York was that ever since the days of King Hudson the four people in York were the Lord Mayor, the Archbishop, the General Officer Commanding and the General Manager of the Railway. They lunched together about once a month. At one of these I was talking about the social upheaval of bringing seven hundred people from London. Archbishop Donald Coggan said: 'Can we help?' And when his diary allowed the Coggans came to each of the railway teas. In fact when the moves had actually been made, almost without exception the Londoners preferred York.

The rest of 1966 went by with me getting evermore petulant with the BRB and through it the Minister for not giving the executive order to move on 1 January 1967. With lightning speed the Board issued the order eleven days before 1 January. We did pretty well to get six people there.

Myself I reflected on how I should go. The fastest and most direct was the 'Towns' line, Kings Cross – Peterborough – Grantham – Doncaster – York. The earlier line was Peterborough – Lincoln — Gainsborough – Doncaster – York. But the earliest was Peterborough – Spalding – Boston – Grimsby – Barton-on-Humber – Ferry to Hull – York.

This last was the route I chose. I think that I had just been reading Grinling's *History of the Great Northern Railway* which I commend to one and all as an account of the costs and difficulties of getting Parliamentary approval for Railway Acts, rival railway schemes, landowners, masters of foxhounds, coal owners even. Still nowadays we should have Friends of the Earth.

It was an enchanting journey. No rush and clatter. Rural railwaymen – incidents of course. The first illustrates, the railway grapevine. At Spalding I was standing on the platform talking to the driver. He finished a packet of cigarettes and threw the empty packet on to the permanent way. I clambered down, retrieved it, handed it back to him. Nothing said. Naturally I didn't tell the story to anyone. But six years later I was at the National Freight Corporation's farewell dinner to George Gibb. My neighbour said: 'Is it true . . . ?' and retold the story. How on earth . . .?

And so in the fullness of time to Barton-on-Humber and a very ancient paddle steamer. Outside the housing of the paddle was a wide sponson on which stood a member of the crew with a pole. He was sounding and needed to. We were churning up acres of mud. But to Hull without stranding and so to York. There was, I thought, a touch of reserve in my reception. It appeared that the Deputy General Manager, Derek Barrie, had strictly enjoined his top management team on parade in the morning, washed behind the ears, clean collars and shirts, pin-stripe suits and a respectful manner. He spent, so he says, all day trying to find out where I was.

I *must* have told Ena what I was doing – or did I?

CONNINGTON: 5.3.67

It was Jean who woke. She nudged me. 'Telephone' she said. It was ringing in the small hours for the first time in the three and a half years since I became a General Manager. Because such were the orders about calls at night, it could mean one thing only, a major disaster to a passenger train. And so Charles Whitworth, 'The 22.30 King's Cross is derailed at Connington. There are several dead.' He went on to tell me who was doing what and going where. 'All right Charles, I'll go over. I'll be there in three hours.'

I dug out Jean's jalopy. Before I left, Harold Few rang with more detail. I set off reflecting how little these things affect me now. They have become professional problems – rescue, clearance of the line, detection of the cause, prevention of a recurrence. Indeed, how remote I had become in that I wasn't going over in my mind the drill of doctors, ambulances, fire service, police and so on. Richard Hardy the local manager would be doing that.

I drove hard through the clear still night and the narrow

Suffolk lanes; Wickham Market, Clopton, Ashbocking. There was not a soul about till I reached Coddenham and an errant curate who inspired me as far as Bury St. Edmunds with song.

'Why' said the people of Coddenham
'Do you preach in your pants? You look odd in 'em.
The bishop will break yer.'
'St. Michael's the maker;
I'll face vicar or bishop or God in 'em.'

I wondered what Marks and Sparks would do with that; nothing I decided.

At Bury the police stopped me. 'Who? Where? Why?' I said: 'General Manager Eastern Region British Railways. To Connington. Accident'. 'Nothing' said the Sergeant 'could be fairer than that' and flashed his lamp into every corner of the car. My credibility rating wasn't high and even to me it sounded highly improbable. The little car took me through Cambridge in under two hours and to the top of Alconbury Hill half an hour later. I stopped there to locate Connington on a quarter-inch map which I couldn't and then to stand on a high point and look for the lights which I knew must be round the wreck. On I went and after a little came to Connington North. They were finishing clearing up there. The front of the train, people unaware at the time that the rear had been wrecked, had gone forward. The second of the two following coaches which had both been partly derailed was being put away into the sidings. 'That's five pitches-in we've had round here in not so long' said the relief signalman on duty. We went round this thought for a little: two slight rear-end collisions, one of which unluckily fouled the next line and resulted in a shambles each from a different cause, a derailment of a freight train on the slow line and now this high speed wreck of an express on the main. 'There's no pattern in that lot' I said. 'Who's the Jonah? Do we need a witch hunt?' 'Not with another Witch Doctor' said a voice from somewhere.

I went on to Connington South where four coaches lay on their side. The leading bogie had been flung 170 yards ahead of its coach; three others had been torn off and lay in a heap at the rear end of the second. The cranes from King's Cross and New England had their snouts high in the air. Drifting steam and musical drum of wheels obedient to a rare whistle told of their lift and set down. Never with coaching stock I have I seen such brilliant breakdown work. Brooks of King's Cross and Addy of New England planned in unison roll and pull and lift. Although the buckeyes were jammed and the buffers locked, each coach at the whistles eased sweetly from the next and was put gently and without fuss on the grass on the far side of the Up Main.

Indeed only once have I seen breakdown work of any kind to match it. That was at Soham in, maybe, 1941 when a train of empty petrol tanks ran headlong through the facing traps. Harry Ball of March it was with his little old 15 ton crane. At the start he couldn't get past Norwich who were also there at work on the leading two open wagons. Norwich that day weren't in very good form. It took them nearly two hours of picking up and putting down in the same place. Harry walked nearly to Barway about five times muttering an unknown language. At last Norwich were clear. 'Now' said Harry 'you ——— off home' and rerailed seventeen tanks in fifty-eight minutes.

The false dawn peered over the Fen. It became bitterly cold. I went into the Accident van's Mess Room for cups of strenuous tea. I demanded the usual corned beef sandwich and was given instead sweet biscuits. Nationalisation again. As the pale light grew Edwin Howell and I set off to walk to Connington North to look at the two carriages which had been put in the siding there. We were interested in the trailing buckeye head of the second which had been found in the dropped position with the support pin out and the lower jaw fractured. We looked at it top, bottom and sides. I said: 'Why is it that the buffers and the vestibule end show no signs of rubbing? If it was running even for a second derailed next to that one which ended on its side, there would be marks.' Then we talked about the fracture. It could have happened while the carriage was bumping along with the front end of the train after the breakaway; or during rerailing; or it could have happened in the main wreck, perhaps as the prime cause. It was now full light. I said: 'We can soon dispose of two of the arguments. If the missing piece is between here and the wreck it can't have been a prime cause. I'll walk back and look'. I didn't find it. I charged everyone on the site to search and soon Adams picked it up wide of the Down slow line opposite the second coach on its side.

Meanwhile Colin Morris had been walking back for a mile searching for any fractured material, axle boxes, springs, and so on. In a wreck like this you must look for every clue everywhere. In the wreck itself so much is torn off and missing that you seldom can tell what is a cause and what a consequence. Colin also had found nothing. Therefore from the conclusions of both ends the evidence of the cause was within a hundred yards.

We looked at the track. We found firstly a tiny distortion of the tip of the blade of the facing points from Main to Slow. This was rusty. A few feet beyond was the first mark of derailment, one wheel leading fairly sharply away from the Main. A few yards further the nose of a diamond crossing was burred and sliced. Beyond this point on one sleeper there were well defined marks of eight wheels on a sleeper, side by side. Then the whole track spread and broke up. In all accidents this work is the most fascinating. So far we had a coupler head in a wrong position and fractured: A rusty and distorted tip on a facing point: a blow on the nose of a crossing: and many axleboxes and other gear missing from the bogies. Which was the cause and which the effect? I got as far as being sure that the first mark of derailment, because the distortion on the facing point was rusty, was a red herring.

At 9.15 I said to Richard 'I'm off to Peterborough to look in at the hospital and wish them well; then to York.' Someone brought him a message. He glanced at it. 'From the BRB's Research Department' he said. His eyes travelled slowly over the line of coaches deposited on the grass, over the rank of separated bogies, round to the wide trench cut by the dozer along the Down Main line and to the distorted rails stacked by the side of the Down slow, then back to the crews of the accident vans who had reached the euphoric and well-deserved stage of self-congratulation which immediately precedes packing up to go. Then his eyes, drained of all emotion, met mine: 'The message from the Research Department says 'Touch nothing till I come' '.

SAFETY

No reflections on railways should omit the subject of safety. It should be in the forefront of Managers' minds and indeed there is a very solid and intricate organisation to see to it.

Railways are not a safe form of transport. Consider driving 400 tons at 150mph along a couple of rails which must not deviate in gauge or in vertical lift, driven by a man who cannot stop in less than a mile and a half.

The engineers, mechanical, civil and signalling have done an outstanding job in raising the parameters of speed from about 75 to getting on towards 150mph in providing the infrastructure to match the speed and in affording the driver the safeguards to enable him to drive safely at those speeds.

On the way there have been one or two slips. In 1962 when I was Chief Operating Officer we began to suffer a real George Stephenson phenomenon. Four-wheeled freight wagons began to derail on plain track. First a pallet van in East Anglia; then a banana van in the Midlands. Then . . . curiously enough the Great Northern was free. One a month – two a month. Then in April twelve. I called a meeting of mechanicals, civils and operators. 'Diesel traction' they said. But I pointed out that twenty-five per cent of the derailments were behind steam traction. We had to take it seriously, not only because some of the wagons ran half a mile breaking every sleeper on the way but if the wagons got in the V of a pair of points or hit a bridge it would spill itself over the opposite line and set up a major accident. Eventually I said: 'We are getting nowhere. We will take a George Stephenson decision. From to-night we will reduce the maximum speed of freight trains from 55 to 45mph. Almost a year later my successor brought it down to 40. Certainly we had no major

Picking up the pieces: cranes clearing the wreckage of the Peterborough–Liverpool Street mail train which in fog ran into the back of a freight train between Kelvedon and Witham on the Colchester main line on 7 March 1950.

disasters for five years. But – what a way to take a decision.

Nevertheless they can go wrong. In 1944–47 I was District Superintendent at Stratford. Our people had had six years of war and were exhausted beyond belief. But good young men were being demobilised. The Chief Signals Inspector and I and the relevant Stationmaster reviewed every signalman in the District to see whether he should be moved – without loss of pay – to the Thames Wharf Branch which had a freight only service. At Romford was Harry Looker, 55 years of age. The stationmaster produced his service history – a clear sheet. The Inspector had examined him recently with good results. Then the stationmaster said: 'Nothing wrong with Harry except maybe he is getting a bit slow.' Now Romford had all the electrical safeguards which we renewed at that time. We decided to leave him there. One foul, foggy night in January 1946 Harry got 'Train running away on right line' from Crowlands, two miles in rear. By the time Harry had picked up his detonators and got to the top of the steps the Haughley Mail was streaking past his signals at danger and two minutes later ran into the rear of a Southend just starting from Gidea Park Station. That one was mine. Harry *was* too slow.

The next derailment on plain track which we had in 1967 is worth a comment for the way it shows up railwaymen. A cement train was lumbering along on the slow line near Thirsk. The 12.00 Kings Cross to Newcastle was streaking down the main line behind. Suddenly four hundred yards ahead mushroomed a cloud of dust. Driver Jones of Gateshead threw out all the anchors. He hadn't a chance. From the dust emerged two wagons, eighty tonnes, on their sides. The express hit them at about 40mph, tearing out the left side of the locomotive and the sides of six carriages. Six people died. At the last moment Jones threw himself on to the fireman's side and was no more than shaken. Meanwhile fireman Smith with probable death 40 seconds away had opened the offside door of the cab, bent down, taken three detonators from his bag and clamped himself on so that if he survived he could run forward and protect the opposite line. When, gentle readers, you think what unreasonable people Ray Buckton and his tribe are remember that these are the sort of people you are talking about. I got to Thirsk about an hour later and talked to the two. Then thinking, wrongly as so often, I was doing them a good turn I sent them off home in my car. Somewhere short of Darlington the brakes failed and they ended up in a field. 'Take us to the nearest station' they cried 'where we can get on a safe form of transport.'

Now to other things. In my experience I have had a lot of 'one-offs'. A train rolling down a bank when the track had not been properly fettled, a deliberate derailment of an express at high speed by a schizophrenic signalman; a water scoop falling off an engine and sticking in the truss bar of the first coach and derailing it; a signal linesman testing terminals and allowing one end of his lead to touch the circuits controlling some junction points so that the first part of the train went to Cambridge and the other half to Colchester; a locomotive crew at Didcot being told by the signalman to 'set back', which being tender first they did straight through a train of petrol tankers, fourteen of which went up in a sheet of flame.

The causes of these are individual human errors. There is

no pattern. But in one instance there is a pattern and it is the most destructive of all because usually the speed is high, the train is heavy, and when it hits an obstruction that obstruction is a massive one. At the British Railways Board in 1961 I asked our Chief Medical Officer whether the British Medical Council could help to find out why a carefully recruited, intensively trained, supervised and disciplined man should disregard the safeguards of his vigilance control and of his automatic warning system and go blinding along into the back of the train ahead. They promised they would. After eighteen months I was getting petulant. So they came to lunch. 'You will be glad to hear that we have established that 80 per cent of the accidents caused by drivers running past signals are within station limits and are at speeds of less than fifteen miles an hour.' 'Thank you very much. Well, I think I know both the reason and the solution to this.'

The four-wheel wagon problem at its worst; stiff springing on the four-wheel cement wagons led to one of them derailing near Thirsk in 1967, bringing other wagons off and into the path of a closely approaching Kings Cross–Edinburgh express on an adjoining line, wrecking the locomotive, No DP2, derailing several coaches and killing five passengers.

The reasons are human nature, casual, slipshod human nature which however much you select, train, supervise and discipline it will once in a hundred or thousand times literally revert to nature. And there is nothing anyone can do about it. The solution is easy – driverless trains.

One story about a runthrough. On a bright, spring morning in the late 1950s the up Aberdonian ran past the up outer home and up inner home at Welwyn Garden City and ran into the back of a Baldock which had just started away. I got there around 7am and found the Aberdonian neatly laid out on its side, engine and carriages in a straight line; not a window broken on the top side. I walked on to the Baldock about a hundred yards ahead. Immediately behind the last coach with his back to it was an enormous fireman in thigh boots and helmet. I said: 'Good morning.' Not a muscle moved. The Roman Sentry at Pompeii. I walked round the train – came back. 'Good morning.' Not a flicker. Then I noticed that almost touching his calf was a shoe. And we dug out the only fatality. 'No, 'e 'adn't seen it, 'e'd not got eyes in the back of 'is 'ead, 'ad 'e?' Some mothers do have them. Stuart Friend, the feature reporter of the *Evening News* asked if he could be a stretcher bearer. So he got the right rear handle. We had to make it up a short but steep embankment. Half way up the blanket slipped and a pale hand emerged and stroked Stuart's face in an affectionate gesture. The hands don't falter.

The inquiry began predictably.

Driver: 'The outer home was full green light but the inner home was at danger and the Baldock was only about three hundred yards ahead.'

Fireman: 'The outer home was a full green light but the inner home . . .'

Running foreman at Peterborough: 'When I signed Derek in this morning it struck me how well he was looking.'

Anyway, when the signal engineer had done every conceivable test on the signal we found that it was a case of running by and the driver found himself back in the shed. That was not the end of it either. Drivers began to report that the signal was irregularly at green when the inner home was

Trouble on the GN main line when an overnight Aberdeen–Kings Cross train ran by a signal at danger and collided with a Baldock–Kings Cross local train on 7 January 1957. (*British Railways*)

at red. We made the District Superintendent hold an inquiry into each case. After about six within a couple of months two cases appeared when it was obvious they were talking about the wrong signal, both on the down, not the up line. It was a put up job by the driver who was a Big Man in Peterborough Loco. So he stayed in the Loco but do you know that six months later I saw that signal. It had been converted to a colour light.

THE MAKING OF A RAILWAYMAN

The London & North Eastern Railway under Sir Ralph Wedgewood and Robert Bell were the pioneers in the training of Managers. There were three forms of entry; from the clerical staff by competitive examination; from the public school at age eighteen and from the Universities after graduation. Then they sent us as far as possible from home; a Londoner drew Newcastle; a Geordie drew Essex. And they set us off on learning the trades from the tradesmen. First the small station where we worked the booking office and the goods office and went out into the yard to learn how to chain a load of steel and to load eighty trusses of hay or straw in a five

172

plank wagon, sheet and rope it correctly. Once, learning a new art, I rolled a milk churn under a Scottish express and the air was full of whining rockets of steel from the churn and later of the same from District Office. That was at Hatfield. Then learning how to use a shunting pole from shunters in Manchester; how to work a signalbox near Doncaster; how to make steam pipes steam tight; how to build a brick arch and how to wash out a boiler from the boiler smiths at Southend; how to fire a locomotive; how to be a controller in Leeds; how to be a timing clerk at Marylebone.

One advantage was that we remembered. One day 50 years later I stood in the High Court of Justice giving evidence on behalf of the Port of London Authority about a shunting accident.

Trevor Jones QC rose to cross examine:

'Mr Fiennes, you were a Railway General Manager for several years?'

'Yes.'

'And before then you were Chief Operating Officer of British Railways?'

'Yes.'

'And before then since about 1950 were in senior positions in management?'

'Yes.' And by now pretty pleased with myself. Then came:

'So you have forgotten all you ever knew about shunting?'

I said: 'In the corner of this court is a shunting pole. Hand it to me and I will show you how to use it.'

End of that line of questioning.

Indeed I now produce proof. A few years before I had invited an Importance of Brass to inspect our new Instanter Coupling. There we all were in our black bowlers and formal coats. There was a rake of wagons against one of which stood a shunting pole. No shunter. I took the pole, laid the shank under the coupling, aligned the pole across the buffer casting and along my right arm, offered a prayer to Percy Bazers, bowed my body and lifted. The coupling slid sweetly off the hook. Promptly I swung it back on again and knocked it into the shoot position. No mashed thumb.

The LNER reaped two general advantages from its training. The fact that what we knew about the trades allowed us to meet any grade whether individually or in a mess hut or at an evening lecture and talk to them in their own language. The second was – and this may be a complete fantasy – that when in a senior position with a difficult decision to take we felt that we had fifty thousand or so men of goodwill all backing us up.

Finally it was a sure foundation on which we could build the standards of performance; safety, speed, frequency, punctuality, comfort and economy.

ASLEF and BR 1982

Sooner or later – sooner we hope – ASLEF and BR will be working together again. From the point of view of each of them as well as from the nation's point of view it is important that their agreement to resume work should be lasting. It would be naïve to suppose that an agreement conceding three per cent in wages on the one hand and flexible rostering on the other will bring lasting peace. The conflict is deeper than that.

The points at issue in 1982 were relatively trivial. Three per cent, less tax, means little to a driver who is one of the most highly paid craftsmen in the country. Flexible rostering, if the plans of the local management at a principal depot in East Anglia for guards was a guide, means two guards less on the regular roster and two more on the roster for rest days. Such is no salvation for BR.

So what was the conflict all about? Surely things far more basic; on the one hand the principle of the driver's status; on the other hand the prospect of one man in the cab.

In recent years the public, uncontradicted by BR, have been conditioned to think that the work and the responsibility of a driver has been dramatically eased by the change from steam to diesel and electric traction. In terms of working conditions this is true. No longer exposed to the elements, no longer peering along the barrel of a boiler at ill-lit signals, protected partly from collision by the Automatic Warning System, no longer coaxing to reluctant performance an obstinate piece of Victorian machinery. To-day's driver drives in comfort.

Nevertheless, if we want from BR a service of which the principles are safety, speed, frequency, punctuality, comfort and economy the driver on the day contributes far more than all the other grading of railwaymen put together. Toward safety he is continually (well, nearly continually) observing signals and continually looking for danger from, or to events on the track ahead such as trains on other lines, vehicles or people at level crossings, obstructions on the line, whether accidental or deliberate and so on. It is the driver who must react instantly. Toward speed he is the sole custodian of speed. Toward punctuality he maintains or recovers time. The signalman, the guard, the carriage and wagon examiner, the permanent way staff, the signalling technical staff, when they intervene, lose time. Toward comfort, compare the silky starts and smooth braking of a driver from, say, King's Cross or Laira with being driven across Australia where cups of tea took to the air from the shelf – not once but as a regular performance. Therefore as the most important man in BR's business, namely running trains, the driver should be cherished.

It remains to consider how BR should cherish him and so settle not only that dispute but those for the years to come. First BR should recognise that the driver ranks above the other operational grades. As money talks, so the recognition should be financial. BR should make a commitment that drivers should receive a substantial percentage extra in the annual wages round. And I am not thinking about three per cent but between ten and twenty per cent. Drivers should be recognisably an elite.

The second principle is that drivers should be members of an elite union. Certainly ASLEF, disappointed, frustrated, dwindling has behaved badly over the last years. And their cause has not been helped by individual members who have fiddled their claims for payment and put themselves into the same class as guards, ticket collectors, refuse collectors,

CAUTION
LOW HEAD
NO SMO
OR
AKED LIG
IN
GINE
D9012
BRITISH
RAILWAYS

directors and managers. Nevertheless, if ASLEF was submerged in the NUR the slow but unavoidable result will be that drivers will become like guards, ticket collectors and the rest, namely less dedicated to safety, speed, punctuality and comfort. Let us retain ASLEF and convert it into a friend of BR. It will not take a lot of doing. The members are already a dedicated class.

On the other side of the coin what should ASLEF, secure in its future, give to BR and indeed to the nation? Flexible rostering – if you like but let us not pile Pelion upon this molehill. The important concession is that one man should be in the cab of a locomotive and not two. If you ask a driver whether he needs him – second driver, an assistant driver, a second man, a fireman – call him what you will – he will say yes. It is part of his survival kit. The possible loss of 6000 firemen strikes at the existence of ASLEF. But guarantee him ASLEF and he will tell you that he neither needs nor wants a second man in the cab.

Here then is the bargain to be struck. On the one hand recognition that the driver is head of the operating profession and that his Union is secure; on the other that the technical advances in the design of locomotives shall be matched by the principle of one man in the cab. Now is the time to go to the root of the conflict. If we patch yet once again, the seeds of the next dispute will germinate before long.

PADDINGTON REVISITED – 1983

Seventeen years on and the end of an era. The question now hangs over the Western Region whether it can survive as a unit of effective management. The latest re-organisation by the British Railways Board has appointed national 'Sector'

Gerry Fiennes chats to Driver H. C. Brown of Deltic diesel No D9012 *Crepello* before the start of a special high speed proving run to assess timetable feasibility for a 124½min schedule from Kings Cross to Doncaster on 4 April 1966. It was of course pure coincidence that this run was made only a few days before the London Midland Region held its own press demonstration run from Euston to Crewe to introduce its new electric timetable! (*British Railways*) managers. One controls the Inter-City services, one the commuter services, one hopefully the freight services. What is left for the General Manager of Paddington to manage? So the plan for 1984 was to move him to Swindon.

Do not, old Paddington hands and friends of the Great Western, believe in the BRB. As re-organisations come, so re-organisations go. Experience as much as hope has taught us that. Secondly, as a railway consists of geography, a timetable and staff, one only of those ingredients is physically capable of being transferred to Euston House, the timetable, and the reorganisers have not done so. It is the first principle of railway organisation that he who produces the timetable, manages the railway. For these reasons the Western will survive and prosper.

In any event what has happened during the *last* seventeen years has been the responsibility and often the doing of the General Manager at Paddington. And it says a great deal for the massive continuity of the Western that however quickly General Managers come and go, the forward progress has been spectacular by any standards.

Let us consider the Western under the three heads of geography, timetables and staff. The order is of course in reverse order of importance, especially on the Western where Western Man has towered above his contempories. Since the mid-1960s the Western has lost, partly by transfer, partly by the 'Beeching' axe about a thousand miles of route. It now stands at 1855 miles or nearly the average for a Region of one-fifth of British Railways. It is good geography, linking large centres of population in the West Country, South Wales and the Midlands with each other and with London. The centres are 'good railway distances' from London; over a hundred miles for competition with coach and car; less than 300 miles for competition with aircraft. The centres moreover are not in a straight line but quadri-furcated so that at least four Inter-City trains an hour can leave Paddington with prospects of a good load for the West Country, Bristol, South Wales and the Midlands. If any Region has geographically a viable entity for Inter-City services it is the

Western. One last word on geography. Those who have read the Press reports on the Serpell Report but not the report itself, let them relax. Just as the Western in the mid-1960s resisted successfully the earlier 'discussion paper', Dr Beeching's Main Line Red Peril, so it will be with Serpell. People fly kites, but one and all they come down to earth. The railway still exists West of Plymouth, West of Swansea, from Salisbury to Exeter, even the Berks & Hants.

To write that the Western is a sensible geographical entity implies that it can have a sensible timetable. So it can and so it has. Through the timetables of the Great Western and the Western Region there has always run a strong principle, that of pattern. In 1839 the service between Paddington and Maidenhead left on each hour except two between 8.00am and 8.00pm. It didn't, incidentally, tell the passengers how long the journey took. In later years – and Sir Felix Pole is the suspect for an act of charlatanry – the pattern remained; arrival times were published; high speeds were vaunted; but the high speeds were for one train on each route, the Limited, the Bristolian, the Cheltenham Flyer. The rest of the service was slow, not only by comparison with the one Steam Spectacular but with other companies. In the 1960s the pattern remained but the drive was to accelerate the whole service to a *vitesse commerciale*. In terms of competition with the car this had been shown to be an average end-to-end speed of 75mph. It had also been shown that such speeds required 4000 horse power under the bonnet.

This horsepower and therefore these speeds were beyond the 'rude mechanicals' of the 1960s. The London Midland Region with electric traction could average some 72mph. The Eastern with the 3300 hp Deltics around 70. The Western with 2700hp Westerns in the high 60s. However the new timetables of the 1960s brought to the railway a great deal of traffic. Nevertheless better was wanted. Luckily help was just round the corner. In 1962 Dr Sydney Jones, head of BR Research, had come to me, then Chief Operating Officer BR and said: 'Gerry, how would you like a train with a top speed of 150mph which does not have to slow down on curves?' I said: 'Very much – when?' Sydney said: 'About seven years.' 1969. The answer to a prayer because Chief Mechanical Engineer Harrison had just dismissed with scorn my request for 4000 horsepower in a locomotive.

Now, in the Kremlin at that time were certain agnostics who disbelieved in Dr Jones' project for the Advanced Passenger Train by 1969. They went away, bless them, and designed the High Speed Diesel Train which, with its average end to end speeds between 85 and 90mph and more has put us beyond the reach of road competition in speed.

The Western laid claim to the first fleet of HSTs. In the timetable of 1977 the Western went to the top – of Britain, of Europe and almost of the world, being second only to the Japanese Shinkansen.

I was brought up in an environment in which men talked about 'the Bloody Company'. On the Western, fifteen years after nationalisation, men still talked about 'the Company' but never do I recall any of them using the words derogatorily or resentfully. Mind you, I heard 'Bloody Hilton' and 'Bloody Raymond' and no doubt others heard 'Bloody Fiennes' but the Company itself was an object of respect and affection. Rightly so. The Great Western Company had cherished its staff. The loyalty was reciprocal. And after nationalisation Keith Grand had resisted for twelve years the attempts to bring alien practices and alien managers on to the Western. Not only that, he had resisted attempts to reduce the numbers of the staff. And Western Man had responded by continuing the Great Western's tradition of cheerful service to the customer and to the timetable beyond what on other Regions was regarded as the call of duty.

Seventeen years on after Raymond and I began to swing the axe at the staff establishment there are no great changes in the attitudes of the real railwaymen, the drivers, guards, signalmen, staff on the permanent way and in the locomotive depots. Certainly in 1982 the Western, like the other Regions, came out on the strikes called by the ASLEF and NUR, but so they did in the 1920s against the Great Western Railway Company. And they went back to work, may be a little shame-faced, and apologised by producing outstanding results for punctuality. The grades which I have mentioned, thanks to the lack of recruitment over the last ten years, are old hands. Over fifty per cent of the drivers are due for retirement in the next five years so the attitudes date back to the Great Western. But have no fear of the younger entry. Just as with you and me, old hands looked at us and said 'He'll never make a railwayman'. But, you know, by trial and error and a bit of luck that no one rumbled us, we did.

The shortcomings are in the Façade and alas the worst is at Paddington where no longer do you see buttonholes on the barriers – nor indeed until too short a time before the train do you see anyone at all. But – and I know this is a personal view – the Façade does not matter much. A railway is a line (geography) for comfort in the ride, a train (timetable) for speed, puntuality, comfort and Western Man for good Company. We do not want people to hang around stations.

Freight sundries traffic was loaded parcel by parcel into goods wagons. This was the traffic that BR opted out of in the 1960s rationalisations. (*British Railways*)

They get up to all kinds of mischief like the two thousand or so Charlies who each year do themselves an injury by falling up or down stairs at stations – and usually blame us. Once a woman who had crossed her legs coming down a bridge at Liverpool Street wrote: 'I was in a hurry – you always start your trains to time.' *O mea culpa.* The logic of which is to reduce the Façade to a minimum. Away with barriers and away with ticket collectors too. Let us be greeted and clipped with companionable chat by the Guard.

In writing this I would probably have offended Sir John Betjeman, great lover of the Great Western and of things Victorian which are worth preserving. Maybe we have a lesson in Bristol where Brunel's station is preserved as a museum and the operational station no longer has its vaulted, steam-collecting and pigeon-collecting roof.

Now finally let us consider what a streamlined but logical geography, our outstandingly good timetables and lasting Great Western tradition in the important grades have brought the Western Region. Incidentally and digressing for a moment, I omitted to comment on the Managers. Some years ago a future Prime Minister lunched with the British Railways Board. I read (*Trains,* USA) that the memorable remark at lunch was 'If you were any good you would be in private industry.' Well, when I was at Paddington I used to invite industrialists, ministers, MPs and so on to lunch in our senior officers' Mess specifically to show off our team. Few went away without commenting what a cracking good lot they were. The present regime does not suffer by comparison. Nor do their results.

The most remarkable feat for both managers and men is however the fact that they can continue to work together when the managers have reduced the numbers from well over 70,000 in the 1950s to around 20,000 now and of this reduction of 50,000 only 14,000 was due to transfers to and from the LM and Southern.

Since the 1950s the productivity of the staff, measured by numbers divided into train miles has increased by some sixty per cent. Alas that freight traffic has in terms of the Great

Block loads of bulk materials carried in fleets of private owner wagons became a feature of modern BR operation from the 1960s.

Western almost vanished. What would Sir Felix Pole or Keith Grand have said – or done – if Welsh coal was a mere 10.2m tons and steel 3.6m and freight trains ran less than a quarter of the region's mileage? Only the aggregates – compliments of Foster Yeoman at Merehead and elsewhere – are booming with over six million tons.

So it is to the passengers that we turn for cheer. Have you ever met a Chief Passenger Manager with egg on his face because his receipts were 30 per cent above budget? Have you met an operating manager who diagrams his HST sets for 830 miles a day or drivers for over 350 miles a day? Have you met a Divisional Manager who has encouraged the 09.20 from Paddington to Bristol to run to Chippenham, 92 miles in 50 minutes, thereby setting a record for a train in normal service on a normal railway of 111.7 miles an hour? You may, if you hang around Paddington or, Swindon. And thanks to the dedication of those on the Western Region more and more people Go Great Western because the going is good.

7

Preservation Tailpiece

HORSE SENSE: FESTINIOG STYLE

In the dawn of railways Brunel was brilliantly connecting Bristol with London by, for most of its length, a virtually level track. He had no great faith in the capacity of his steam locomotives to climb hills. Indeed for the not-so-level section between Bristol and Swindon he designed a different locomotive. In the fullness of time Brunel's Great Western spread westwards and northwards, accepting the same limitations; but they found that life in Wales was not the same.

The Good Lord has put the coal and slate high in narrow valleys or on the tops of mountains. Following the philosophy of Brunel I have spent a whole day pushing empty coal wagons, five at a time, up the mountain to the Vron colliery. After that we pinned down the brakes on 37 loaded wagons, commended our souls to God and skidded down the mountain until we were safely arrested by the stretch of level track between its base and the junction with the main line.

As Paddington spread onwards and Westward with the need to spell, and less certainly to pronounce words like Machynlleth and Pwllheli, they found that at the same time as Brunel was laying his incomparable railway between Swindon and Paddington the Welsh had a completely different idea. They said 'The Lord has put the slate right up the mountain at Blaenau Ffestiniog. He has in His wisdom allowed the ships to come no further than Portmadoc at sea level. What then is gravity for? What can Sir Isaac Newton do for Wales?' So they built on a gradient of 1 in 80 falling, a railway twelve miles long from the slate quarries of Blaenau Ffestiniog through Tan-y-Grisiau, Dduallt, (a sneeze pronounces this best), Tan-y-Bwlch, Penrhyn, Minffordd and so over the Cob across the estuary to Portmadoc Habour where the schooners and hoys and bawleys were waiting to take the best roofing material in the world to eager markets.

We should interpolate here that the Festiniog spelt with one 'F' was so spelt because the Parliamentary draftsman who drafted the Railway Act could not spell. My brother who is in that line of business and is indeed head of it, says that it must have been some other guy.

So the Festiniog Railway ran trains of slate without locomotives. They had brakesmen on the wagons because 1 in 80 down is an accelerating gradient; and a final wagon called the Dandy in which rode the horse. The purpose of the horse was to pull the empty wagons back up the mountain to Blaenau Ffestiniog. No Welsh mountain ponies, these, but draught horses of immense strength, resource and sagacity.

So on this day Dai and Twm and Huw took a train out of Blaenau and feared no evil. They reeled round the ledges, high above the valleys and sang Cwm Rhondda and Men of Harlech and other patriotic but less printable ditties till the Welkin rang – until indeed they ran out into the Cob at Portmadoc and Dai looked back. 'Where is Blodwen?' he cried. And indeed on the train there was no dandy containing the massive and serene presence and the potential energy of Blodwen.

Now British Railways prudently provides for the event of 'Train divided'. Each train, or light engine, should carry at its rear a tail lamp. If a goods train passes a signalbox without a tail lamp the signalman sends to the box in advance 7 bells 'stop and examine train'. There the signalman stops the train and says to the driver: 'Where's your tail lamp?' If the reply is: 'Tail lamp be damned. Where's me bloody train?' then the signalman knows he is in the presence of not just forgetfulness but of a divided train. This train according to the principles laid down by Sir Issac Newton and aforesaid may either be stopped, if the line is level, or running backwards, or approaching at a rate of knots. So he puts all his signals to danger, clears the engine into a siding, prepares to send the appropriate bell signals and places three detonators ten yards apart on the line so as to alert a possibly somnulent guard.

On the Festiniog the signalman could not put signals to danger because there were no signals; nor put the engine in a siding because there was no siding; nor engine, come to that. Nor was there a signalman. But Huw and Twm and Dai did what they could by putting down detonators and braced themselves for the arrival of Blodwen at 60 plus miles an hour.

After a while it became evident that there was to be no such arrival. So Huw and Twm persuaded Dai – with some difficulty because the next port of call was the Local where there was no closing time then – and indeed not much more now if you know where – to go looking for Blodwen. So Dai plodded up the mountain looking over the edges to see whether Blodwen had gone roly-poly down into the valley. Presently another truck of slate came down. It stopped by Dai. One of the brakesmen said: 'we passed Blodwen in the loop at Tan-y-Bwlch attached to her dandy. What then?' And Dai didn't know what then.

When he reached T-Y-B he found Blodwen standing with her traces attached to the dandy ready for the haul to Blaenau. Dai patted her and said: 'What you been doing, girl?' And she looked at him with a James Thurber expression and said: 'What a way to run a railway'. In Welsh of course.

Dai could make nothing of this without help so he loaded her into the dandy and rode down to Portmadoc where he told Hew and Twm all that had passed. Hew was openly sceptical. 'No horse has spoken' he said. 'She whinnied at you, bach.' 'So I thought at first' said Dai.' So I repeated: 'What you been doing, girl?' and she said again: 'What a way to run a railway.' This time in English. Bi-lingual, she is, and no opinion of me for not understanding Welsh.'

Now Huw was a bit of a sea-lawyer and he said: 'It is provided, is it, in Rule 4 that any unusual occurrence must be reported. Have we here an unusual occurrence?' Dai and Twm maintained a long silence. On the one hand the occurrence was unusual. On the other neither wanted any part in a report. Reports led up all sorts of side alleys with avenues explored and no stones unturned and eventually pages of reprimand with which they had great difficulty because they could not read English, let alone Welsh.

Nevertheless, Huw persisted and was elected not unwillingly to go and see the Manager. The manager heard him to the end and believed every word of the story. He said: 'This is a matter too high for me. We must inform the Board of Directors. What else for have we a Board of Directors?' and Huw didn't know what for they had a Board of Directors whatever.

The Board debated the problem throughout a long day. Not that the principal decision was not clear. They could not have the horses criticising the management with phrases like: 'what a way to run a railway.' The only concession was that they were to be allowed to retire on pension, principally because the Chairman, flown with insolence and wine after lunch, tripped over the words 'Instant Dismissal'. No, the problem was that no Director knew, when all the wagons had travelled loaded down the mountain to Portmadoc, how to haul the empty wagons back up the mountain to Blaenau except by pulling them with a horse. Eventually the Secretary said: 'In England . . .' and was promptly shushed by the Chairman, firstly because secretaries should be seen and not heard and secondly that even in these days of the Welsh Freedom Army there is no freedom of Wales from England as there was in Victorian times. So the fruitless discussion dragged on until at long last the Vice-Chairman said (the Chairman by now being sunk in apathy): 'Mr Secretary, some time ago you were saying . . .' and the secretary held the Board spellbound with the story of James Watt and the kettle, Trevithick and his horseless carriage, Brunel and Stephenson.

So, in 1863, steam came to the Festiniog; *Prince* and *Princess, Merddyn Emrys* more recently *Linda* and *Blanche,* and the *Earl of Merioneth.* The General Manager, because the Festiniog is no longer a truly serious railway paying a steady 8 per cent by the efforts of Dai and Twm and Huw and Blodwen, has his own engine, *Linda,* and may be seen on his way up the mountain to Blaenau, but what is beyond dispute is that while he may have the resource and sagacity of Blodwen (just about) he cannot match her for strength. There is also *Welsh Pony*. But she is stripped down in pieces. For me as a Director she can stay that way. We cannot have her back in service and liable to criticise the management with phrase like: 'What a way to run a railway'. Horses are *out* for fear that they talk out of turn.

ALL THIS AND, NEARLY, HEAVEN TOO

'Bishop, for God's sake, put on that brake!!'

Not many of you have had the opportunity, or the need, to speak so sharply to a prelate. Indeed it would be a surprise if anyone reading this had ever been firemen to a bishop. But if any one has, then, so to speak, this bishop was certainly *that* bishop. Eric Treacy, no less.

He and I had been invited to perform a ceremony on the Middleton Railway. The most dramatic part was to embark on *Matthew Murray* and drive it for the entertainment of a crowd of well-wishers who, when the thing went wrong, were visibly and audibly sorry that it had not gone crashingly wrong.

We paraded. We embarked.

'Will you drive?' said Eric.

I had seen that the fire was well up and bright. So I said:

'No, I'll do the firing' and leant in a negligent attitude on the corner of the cab.

'Right' said Eric. He pulled the whistle cord deafeningly and jerked at the regulator.

We shot off backwards, neither of us having observed that *Matthew* was in reverse gear. And that would not have been so bad if fifty yards away the points had not been set for a siding. Immediately inside it stood a wagon loaded with very solid projecting steel. So . . .

'Bishop, for God's sake put on that brake!!'

Eric laughed all over his face, being maybe more ready to meet his Headquarters upstairs than was a railway general manager. He reached for the nearest thing and jerked it. A deafening whistle again. The next handle was the right one. We slid to a shrieking halt a few yards clear.